INSIDE THE PUB

MAURICE GORHAM

& H. McG. DUNNETT

INSIDE THE PUB

foreword by J. M. RICHARDS

drawings in colour by GORDON CULLEN

THE ARCHITECTURAL PRESS LONDON

The doors are shut, but not bolted or barred—on the contrary, they swing—on patent hinges that give the utmost return for the effort expended, so that one can exchange for the wet pavement and cold wind whatever it is that evokes the mysterious radiance in the engraved glass panels. But what is it? Victorian moralists averred that the pub door was the gate to perdition, but today we begin to see that the Gin Palace was not, and is not, such a wicked place after all. For the dispossessed of the Victorian epoch it gave the only glimpse they were likely to get of a world no longer enslaved to Giant Squalor. Today we realize that it is not only the poor and derelict for whom these portals hold an invitation. They appeal, by methods that have been understood throughout the centuries, to that part of every adult that remains open to thoughts other than those of self-interest, utility, practical politics and expediency. They are the portals to the world of fantasy, and if the process of getting oneself unattached is sometimes earthy, that is society's fault and not the Gin Palace's. In front of these doors we are, in fact, in the presence of *Art*, of a robust and popular, yet nevertheless noble, kind—Rubens, not Botticelli. This book deals with the more sober aspects of the pub tradition—of the pub vernacular. Let this frontispiece (and five other pages in the book) celebrate the great virtues of Gin Palace art. Let these words do something to arrest the wanton destruction of engraved glass, gilt lettering, gasoliers, brasswork on ram's head tables, cast ironwork, and brewers' trade-marks.

ACKNOWLEDGEMENTS

The authors and publishers acknowledge with thanks the valuable help and advice, in the preparation of this book, given by Mr. Gerald Millar, secretary of the Advisory and Development Council of the Brewing Industry. They also acknowledge their indebtedness to Barclay, Perkins & Co.; Courage & Co.; Mitchells and Butlers Ltd.; Truman, Hanbury, Buxton & Co.; Watney, Combe, Reid & Co.; Whitbread & Co.; Mr. J. W. P. Groves, director of the N.T.D.A. Staff Education Committee and Mr. W. R. Dobbs, of Gaskell and Chambers Ltd., for information on pub development; to Mr. John Clark, director of James Clark and Eaton Ltd.; Mr. J. C. Corsan, director of The London Sand Blast Decorative Glass Works Ltd.; and Mr. K. Underhill, director of Evans & Co. (Glaziers) Ltd., for details of decorated glass techniques; to The Wall Paper Manufacturers Ltd., for the history of embossed wall coverings; to Mr. Zephaniah Carr for an account of graining and marbling; to the British Museum Print Room; to the Guildhall Library; and to the Victoria and Albert Museum.

Grateful acknowledgement is also made for illustrations as follow:
Edward Ardizzone, 21; Barclay Perkins & Co., 33; B. T. Batsford Ltd., 23; Charles Borup, 139, 140; British Museum, 2, 4–10, 45, 52, 55; G. W. Dunton, 88, 89, 123; de Burgh Galwey, 1, 44, 49, 69, 76–7, 81–3, 85–7, 94–8, 100–1, 103–6, 110, 115, 119, 124–8; Wilson Gould, 129; Guildhall Library, 3, 13–15, 18, 19, 22, 47, 56, 66; Home Office, 31; Lewis & Randall, 30, 41; John Maltby, 75, 84, 113–4, 116–8; Percival Marshall, 17, 27–9; H. A. Mason, 134; Gerald Millar, 24; Millar & Harris, 137; Sydney W. Newbery, 138, 141; Newcastle Breweries Ltd., 93; by courtesy of Miss Violet Oliver, 130, 131; Philipson, 133; *Picture Post*, 35–7, 58, 135–6; E. R. H. Read, 40; by permission of André L. Simon, 57; Humphrey Spender, 34, 78–80, 99, 102, 107–9, 111–2, 121, 122; Marguerite Steen, 16; Edwin W. Taylor, 32; Travel Association, 53; Truman, Hanbury, Buxton & Co., 67; Victoria & Albert Museum, 11, 43, 71–4; A. C. K. Ware Ltd., 48, 50, 51, 54, 90–2, 120; Watney, Combe, Reid & Co., 68; R. L. Watson, 42.

First published 1950
Printed and bound in Great Britain by W. S. COWELL LTD, Ipswich

CONTENTS

ILLUSTRATIONS

8

9

FOREWORD

If I were asked what are the qualities I would like to find in a pub I would say simply, 'the right atmosphere', and if asked to be a little more precise I would say that the right atmosphere is one which provides warmth, cheerfulness and a sense of seclusion and one in which the charm of the familiar is somehow combined with a sense of something intriguing just round the corner. A pub should make people feel at home and yet have the capacity to lift them a little out of themselves.

Now qualities of this kind are among the most difficult for architects to contrive, because they depend on something far less tangible than the harmonious proportions, the logical planning and the right use of materials which are supposed to be the attributes of good architecture. These only come into the picture in so far as they contribute to the general effect which, moreover, to be properly appreciated must not seem to have been too consciously designed.

For this reason the pub—especially its interior—has proved to be one of the knottiest architectural problems of our age. The problem which is posed here more vividly than anywhere else is how to establish an architecture which is modern in the sense of belonging to its own time—which takes full advantage of contemporary techniques and materials—but yet is firmly rooted in the needs and responses of ordinary people, giving them what they have a right to demand of their environment—an architecture progressive without being inhuman and popular without being silly.

In the pub this last conflict is the most difficult to reconcile. That it should be popular is the very essence of the purpose of the pub; if it cannot be this it might as well not exist. But its popularity depends largely on its possessing that familiar atmosphere already referred to, and thus on the existence of a tradition, and it is but a short step from the conservation of tradition to the attempted imitation of the antique. The mock-Tudor and mock-Georgian styles which have been so prevalent in contemporary pub design have sprung, therefore, from a genuine attempt to seek out qualities to which the public is most ready to respond. But a misguided attempt; clearly they represent an evasion of the real problem, and this has been proved by their failure to achieve a genuine pub atmosphere.

Equally clearly the architects' efforts to design modern pubs have not succeeded any better. Contemporary design, because it has no popular idiom to work in, has become an *ad hoc* process and its results have not the advantage of appearing inevitable and immediately familiar. Even a skilful piece of design, by a sensitive and intelligent architect, does not necessarily produce a good pub interior. Add to this the attempts by some pub designers to replace the specious glamour of the mock-Tudor by the equally specious glamour of chromium steel and jazz-modern (which may produce good night-clubs but not good pubs) and the unfortunate effects of 'improved' pub planning, and we can see the reason for the failure of most of the new-style pubs. The improvements that pub owners are constantly trying to make are no doubt desirable on grounds of hygiene, convenience and a high standard of service and supervision, but they cannot afford to ignore the intangible visual attributes on which the appeal of the pub rests. It must be insisted again and again that good pub design consists in creating the right visual atmosphere, and that (to give but one example) to sacrifice the old and cosy multiplicity of bars for one large one where the sense of intimacy is lost, all to placate the magistrates' passion for supervision, is a betrayal of the pub tradition.

What is required, then, is to discover ways and means of recreating the familiar atmosphere of the traditional pub without resorting to period copyism. Before this can be done it is necessary to examine the pub tradition, to see how it evolved, of what it consists, to what extent it is a live, continuing tradition and, finally, to what extent its ingredients are such as can be absorbed into the modern architectural idiom. That was the task—a task, strangely enough, never attempted before—which the editors of *The Architectural Review* set themselves when they decided recently to devote a special number to the subject of pub interiors, and that is the purpose of this book, which is a rearrangement of the material contained in the special number of *The Architectural Review*.

Throughout these pages the assumption is maintained that a contemporary pub must be a piece of contemporary architecture. Nevertheless, they show quite clearly that much can be learnt from the pub tradition in order that the atmosphere so effectively created in the past can be recreated in a modern way. For the things that are important about pub interiors are, on the whole, quite independent of the architectural styles current when they were built. A good Tudor pub is not good on account of its black oak beams and the leaded lights in its windows, any more than a good Victorian pub is good simply on account of its carved mahogany screens and the engraved glass in

12

its windows. In spite of their superficial differences, they are both good because of what they have in common, rather than because of whatever links them with one particular period. And *The Architectural Review*'s researches proved that the things they have in common, the methods used to create a sense of warmth and friendliness in old pubs—of whatever period—are equally valid today: the close and intricate subdivision of large rooms to give a feeling of seclusion and intimacy, the use of glass screens and mirrors to give mystery and sparkle, the use of rich dark colours, the use of bottles and barrels and brewers' trade-marks as decoration.

These can all be legitimately used in modern designs, and to build anew on the basis of whatever remains valid of the old is always the business of the architect. In coming years there will be great activity in pub building, to make up for those lost during the war and to provide the amenities only the pub can offer in the new towns and other newly built-up areas. That will be an opportunity of showing how the no-doubt necessary improvement in the standard of pub planning and service can be combined with a respect for the English pub tradition, not because of what it was in the past, but because of deep need of it today, of showing what the improved pub of recent years has lost by turning its back on the great mass of popular art which it inspired. The art of the pub is one of the few living arts which is still popular in a spontaneous, unself-conscious way. May this book help to ensure that its real nature is understood, valued and put to good use.

J. M. RICHARDS

*ll∙ nigtlun quôus∙ con
doicium∙ et icq' illicitc*

THE PUB AND THE PEOPLE *by* Maurice Gorham

*Pub architecture has evolved as the part played by the pub in English life
has developed and changed. In this chapter drinking and drinking habits—the
places where people drink in public, the laws that control their drinking
and the social customs that condition it—are described as a continuous
story that begins in the medieval alehouse kitchen and must be left unfinished
in the modern lounge bar and road house. The story is illustrated by
pictures of pub life and the people who created it throughout its history.
Above is the first known pub illustration, a roadside alehouse from* The
Smithfield Decretals, *early fourteenth century, with the traditional bush
over the door, the ancestor of the inn sign.*

Like most ancient institutions, the English pub has gathered around itself a
mass of superstitions, false impressions, unfounded claims, so that it is constantly praised or blamed for no longer being what it never was. Even the
present-day pub that we can see at every street-corner is still wrapped in a
haze of misrepresentation, due sometimes to ignorance, sometimes to propa-
ganda, sometimes to sheer sentiment. To listen to the brewers you would

think the pubs were the chief hope of the social future; the temperance people talk of them as if they were chemists' shops licensed to dispense poison without using the Poison Book; to read a debate on pubs in Parliament you would sometimes imagine the pubs they were discussing were on another planet. The film producers have added to the confusion by building pub sets that would have seemed anachronistic to Arthur Morrison. It is only recently that one has begun to sit up in the one-and-ninepennies and say, as a new scene came on, 'Ah yes, that's the *Star Tavern* in West Belgrave Mews'.

The clash of interests over the present-day pub has coloured our view of pubs of the past. One side thinks immediately of gracious coaching inns with mine host beaming ruddily as he carries in the smoking roast, the other thinks of 'dead drunk for twopence' and the evil dens of the Ratcliffe Highway. The truth surely is that the pub has always meant different things to different men, so that there has always been more than one type of pub, and in each category there have been good pubs and bad. Roughly speaking, it looks as though the pubs reached their highest level in the heyday of road travel before the railways came in, and their lowest in the Victorian industrial age. But this is speaking very roughly indeed, and it is hardly possible to average out so multifarious a product as the English pub.

DEFINITIONS

Before we go further, let us define what we are talking about. The word 'English' is used here deliberately and not by oversight. The pub is primarily an English rather than a British institution, and though it is to be found in other parts of the British Isles and even beyond, it is in England that it is most firmly rooted and that it reflects the drinking habits of the people as closely as do the cafés of Paris or the bars of New York. And the term 'public house', or 'pub', is here used not in its strict legal sense but generally for a place where you can buy a drink and drink it without the obligation to do anything else, such as buying a meal or dancing or booking a room. This is the sense in which the word is commonly used, and in most people's vocabulary a pub is hardly a pub unless the choice of drinks includes draught beer. You may be able to get all sorts of other things in a pub, from a bottle of champagne to poetry readings, from a cheese roll to a room for a week, but the common denominator is the liquor that you buy and drink.

From the first there seems to have been this plurality about the pub, the rough division being into the alehouses where the customers came to drink beer, the taverns where they came to drink wine, and the inns where they

16

came to spend the night. The categories overlapped, of course, and you could usually spend the night in the alehouse even if you could not get a bed, but you could always get a drink in the inn.

THE LAW OF THE PUBS

The pubs grew up with the towns and villages and high-roads, and they were affected by ordinary social and economic factors as were houses and shops; but from the first they were also the subject of special attention from the law. Laws are not always enforced and we cannot expect to find in the Statute Book a life-like representation of the pub as it really was, but let us look first at the sort of pub these laws were trying to produce.

Enactments to regulate the sale of liquor began even before there was a Parliament to pass them, and went on throughout the Middle Ages. The inns, taverns, and alehouses were subject to the type of legislation applied to all forms of buying and selling, designed to ensure that the customer got value for his money, and to legislation aimed to prevent disorder, night-walking, and unlawful games (for the pubs, like football, could distract men from the proper patriotic practice of archery). But there are also early indications of the desire to prevent tippling, which again foreshadows a lot of legislation nearer to our own times.

The modern note is first struck, perhaps, in the Statute of 1552 by which the licensing of alehouses was put into the hands of Justices of the Peace, who usually granted the licence for one year; longer licensing was expressly forbidden by the later Proclamation of 1618. As the Royal Commission of 1932 said, this statute is the foundation of all our legislation concerning the sale and consumption of intoxicating liquor, and subsequent legislation is mere amendment.

Throughout the seventeenth century the law continued to discourage tippling. Alehouses were officially regarded as being primarily for wayfarers and for those who could not get cooked meals at home; at one time tipplers were limited to one hour in the pub, and a multiplicity of alehouses was frowned upon then as later. In 1623, for instance, the Justices in Ripon came to the conclusion that the town had too many alehouses and reduced the number by half. There is no record that compensation was paid for the licences thus rudely extinguished; we have to wait until the present century for that. After the Restoration in 1660 the laws against tippling ceased to be enforced. At the same time duties on liquor began to be an important source of revenue to the Crown, the drinking of spirits became popular, the taverns spread fast.

17

From now on the fear of spirit-drinking as a social evil leaves its mark on the laws about drink.

The most important enactment for the future was, however, that of 1729, which made it necessary for the Justices' licence to be granted at a general meeting of the local Justices, instead of by two Justices who might have no connection with the locality and no knowledge of its needs. This Act, complementing the Statute of 1552, set the pattern for licensing procedure up to the present day.

However virtuous the liquor laws might be, eighteenth-century Justices were hardly the people to enforce them. The later eighteenth century was an age of licence (using the word in its wider sense) and London in particular became what was later to be known as a 'wide-open town'. The Wesleyan movement brought a new effort towards sobriety, and the Royal Proclamation of 1787 resulted in numerous restrictions—closing times, Sunday closing, refusal of new licences, and suppression of existing public houses and dram shops. The next great Consolidating Act was passed in 1828—before Parliament was reformed—and this Act repealed all previous legislation and remained the basis of licensing law until 1910. Notably it confirmed the annual licence, removed the power of the Justices to suppress a licence at any time, provided for transfer of licences at dates between the annual licensing sessions, and fixed the Justices' licence and the two excise licences, one for ale, beer, cider and perry, the other for wines and spirits. No licence was needed for off-sales.

Meanwhile, however, gin-drinking had been increasing to an alarming extent, and one reason for this was found in the growth of the tied-house system, by which one brewery had a monopoly of supplying one pub, this being alleged to result in the supply of inferior beer. The Beerhouse Act of 1830, which made it legal for anybody to sell beer for consumption on or off the premises without a licence from the Justices, was intended to break both the gin habit and the brewers' tie, but it failed to do either. Instead, it led to an orgy of beer-drinking, tremendous promotion of sales by the brewers, the rise of the 'splendid gin-shops' described by Dickens, as a counter-attraction to the beerhouses where spirits could not be sold. In 1869 the licensing of beerhouses was restored to the Justices (with a special provision about ante-1869 licences which has only recently ceased to apply) and off-licences were also brought under their control.

The rest of the nineteenth century foreshadows the controversies of the twentieth. The line of battle was already drawn up. On the one side stood the Nonconformist Conscience, newly armed with political power; on the other

18

the brewing industry, now grown into a nation-wide interest, largely as a result of the tied-house system which the Act of 1830 had failed to shake. A significant test of power came in 1871, when Gladstone's Government withdrew its Licensing Bill after furious opposition had been organized by the Trade, with the temperance people opposing it as well. There were various enactments which have had lasting effect—the right of ordinary removal, the six-day licence and early-closing licence, Sunday closing in Wales—but the great event of the end of the century was the Royal Commission of 1896–99. By this time the brewers, with their strong financial interest in licensed premises, were beginning to challenge the right of the Justices to suppress licences on grounds of redundancy, without regard for the loss involved. The stage was set for the conflict over compensation that makes the licensing law of the twentieth century so different in its essentials from that of any earlier age.

WHAT THE PUBS WERE LIKE

Former centuries were less fully documented than ours, and we could wish that Chaucer had given us as full a description of the *Tabard* in Southwark as he has of its host. Time and change have taken away all but fragments of the old inns. There are a great many pubs claiming antiquity, but very few of them retain much of their original character, and this applies even to pubs of the last two hundred years. Sometimes you find that restoration and demolition have spared a range of windows or even a whole front, more often only the original cellars, or a doorway, or a carved sign; sometimes the house parades its traditions although it has been entirely rebuilt. Even the architectural historian has to call on a good deal of imagination to reconstruct the famous inns as they really were when they were built.

To begin with the exterior, we can gather that for a long time the local alehouse and the small inn looked much the same as the houses that surrounded them; the pub, like the shop, was slow to acquire an appearance of its own. The alehouse might indeed be primarily a private house in which you could buy a drink in the kitchen, and this character still clings to many a country pub despite the specializing pressure of the licensing system. Even the bigger inns, which made a point of display, looked very like the houses of rich merchants and sometimes of gentlemen, and many of them have in fact become private houses in the course of time. Before the days of brewers' advertisements the inn or tavern must have been distinguished mainly by its sign; hence the elaborate and beautiful signs, sometimes across the road facing the pub, sometimes completely spanning the roadway, of some of the big highroad houses, and the humble bush on a staff that drew the wayfarer's attention to the cottage where the goodwife would sell him a pot of beer. The house itself would usually be in the same style as its neighbours, the prevailing style of its place and time. Where the old inn looks very different from its surroundings it is because it has survived them. Apart from the commercial advantages of antiquity in a pub, which are not always recognized, the legal restrictions about rebuilding them did much to keep them anachronistic, but until the nineteenth century we can find few whose external architecture must have conveyed unmistakably, when they were built, that they were public houses and not private houses or cottages or farms.

The resemblance applies to the interior too. So far as it is possible to generalize, we may say that public houses up to the mid-nineteenth century aimed mainly at reproducing the amenities of the home. They would naturally try to improve on them and they might even run to assembly-rooms and ball-rooms such as no customer would be likely to have in his own home; other-wise, of course, he would not need to go to the inn. But except for the dining-room of the city tavern, with its separate boxes, there seems to have been no room in a traditional inn so different from a room in a private house as was, say, the Victorian saloon bar.

As the original categories of alehouse, tavern, and inn gradually fused, so the three types of pub that we now know began to emerge. From the first there were pubs that tried simply to provide the atmosphere of a 'Home from Home', and pubs that tried to be obviously 'Grander than Home'. The third type, the pub whose appearance and appeal were 'Frankly Theatrical', came later with the growth of cities and the need to appeal to a casual trade. Ulti-mately of course these three also tended to overlap, so that you can now find pubs that provide a home from home in the public, a private or saloon that is like home but grander, and a frankly theatrical touch in the winter garden or saloon lounge.

Originally the smaller inns and alehouses were laid out much like a private house, as they often are in the country to this day. Even now the bar is not universal; often you go into a room that might be an ordinary cottage living-room, though it is no longer also used as a kitchen, take your place on a settle in front of the fire, and give your order to somebody who appears at the door and then goes away to get the beer from some unseen source. In this sort of pub, if you are a guest whose social standing obviously demands special treatment, you will be shown into an icy parlour, furnished exactly like the show-parlour of a small house. This domesticity seems to have been even more marked in the past, when the common-or-garden customer normally drank in the kitchen of the inn, amongst the coming and going of the family and the staff, and often slept there after the family had gone off to bed. Furniture and fittings followed ordinary domestic styles, from oak to deal and mahogany. The one refinement that you would not expect to find was a carpet on the floor; this, for obvious reasons, would be reserved for that later development, the landlord's own little parlour into which only favoured clients were allowed. As time went on the patrons often turned this bar parlour into just another drinking compartment, though still a select one, and the landlord retired elsewhere, so that in many modern pubs his office is in a one-man cubby-hole at the back of the bar and his private sitting-room upstairs.

From the first, however, we find the other type of house which set out to provide something grander than the patron normally had at home. This might be either the tavern or the inn. Professor Richardson's reconstruction of the *Mermaid Tavern* in Cornhill in 1420, soon after Chaucer's time, shows us a big lofty room under an open-timbered roof with screen and gallery, with a log fire blazing on the stone hearth, and oaken tables scattered here and there, at which the patrons sat drinking the blackjacks of strong ale, Rhenish wine in silver mazers, and bottles of Bordeaux, brought to them by the drawers from cellars where they were carefully counted out by the cellarers using their tally-sticks. Making due allowances for the changes of five centuries, this seems to me not at all unlike the big bar at *Henekey's* in High Holborn, where the medieval style has been reproduced with more than usual success. Take away the long bar-counter down one side, strew the floor with well-trodden rushes amongst which dogs and rats snuffle for bones, and you might well be going into a fifteenth-century tavern when you penetrate into that long high-raftered hall; all the more so if they would only borrow those heavy oaken doors, iron-studded, swinging on strap hinges, from *Henekey's* in the Strand.

The bigger inns and taverns had from the first to cater for business meetings and formal entertainment as well as for private conviviality. In the time of Edward I the wool-traders of Norton St. Philip had the upper room of the *George* reserved for their use, and in later ages the coaching inns and the big taverns of the country towns had dining-rooms, assembly rooms, and ball-rooms in which parties could meet and private people could entertain as they could not do at home. This use, of course, thrives heartily today. Except for the new pubs built as part of a pile of flats or an office block, most pubs rise three or four storeys from the ground, and nearly all of them have upper rooms in which parties and clubs can meet. Sometimes they are the dining-rooms that are open to the public at lunch-time, sometimes they are separate suites. Many a club and benevolent society holds all its meetings in the upper room of one or other of the local pubs.

Besides these there were the private apartments for travellers, which formed an important side of the activities of the larger inns. These were of all varieties from magnificent rooms such as that in the *Angel* at Grantham, in which a king could stay, to the cheerless draughty bedrooms that so many eighteenth-century travellers have described. Many such travellers fled from the struggling fires, newly lighted when they arrived, and the sombre bed-hangings of the best room and took their candle down to the kitchen, where the locals and the servants were drinking happily over a roaring fire.

As for the people who kept the inns and served in them, there is plenty of conflict in the evidence about them. Nowadays it is a fashion to yearn for the days when mine host was the friend and confidant of everyone who used his house, but calling him mine host does not alter the fact that then he could be far more of a tyrant and an extortioner than he possibly can now. The jovial landlord of tradition pops in and out of the records but so do the surly landlord, the cheating landlord, and the landlord whose welcome is too obviously measured by his estimate of the length of your purse. We have said that inns probably reached their highest level in the coaching age, but it is in this very age that we have most evidence of the landlord who seemed to believe that travellers who would not be coming there again anyway were fair game. This is partly because the picaresque novels dwelt naturally on the mishaps of travellers, especially poor travellers, but there seems to have been every chance of ending a night in an inn with a row with the landlord, if not a stand-up fight with the whole staff, and the long series of legal enactments on the duties of inn-keepers affords some grounds for thinking that in the days of slow travel and lack of alternatives, the landlord had every temptation to exploit the benighted unless he were firmly restrained by the law.

The staff of an inn or tavern could vary as it does now. A small alehouse might be kept by the man and his wife with one servant, and the wife might do most of the serving during the day whilst the husband worked outside. A big inn catering for travellers could have a large and miscellaneous staff. The medieval drawer in his leather apron and tight round cap gave way to the inn waiter for whom so few travellers had a good word to say. The waiter at Yarmouth, who ate David Copperfield's dinner and drank his half-pint of ale, was only doing on his own account what many coaching inns did scientifically to travellers with a limited stay. They made a practice of bringing the dinner so late and so hot that their guests could eat hardly any of it before the fresh horses were in and the coachman was clamouring to be away.

A big inn which supplied horses to the stage-coaches or kept horses for posting would have a large outside staff. Besides the waiters and chamber-maids and cooks there would be a corps of ostlers and maybe post-boys, and they, with the servants of wealthy travellers and the general hangers-on of the stables, would form the main custom of the tap-room which can still be found somewhere at the rear of most old hotels. Inside, the drinking would be mainly at tables or in the separate rooms to which superior travellers retired. The bar would be a dispense or place for serving, not drinking. The drinking-bar seems to be a comparatively modern development in the plan of the pub.

The big inns were the show-pieces of the licensed trade, but all over the country you would still find the small houses such as Morland drew, where the country folk and the humbler wayfarers dropped in for their drink, and some of these wayside houses are still there to this day. On the Yorkshire moors, in the lanes of Oxfordshire, even in the old villages round London you can still find those little houses, set back a bit from the by-road, with a sign on the far side of the way, a couple of benches and tables outside and a couple of deal settles inside, where the local people drink their ale and talk slowly about the affairs of the neighbourhood as they always did. But the house may bear the advertisements of a big brewery now, and the bus from the corner may take people off to the Woolworth's and Odeons of the nearest town, maybe to be seduced there by the strip-lighting and pin-tables of the latest improved modern licensed house.

NINETEENTH CENTURY

The nineteenth century brought great changes in the pubs, as it did through-out the social scene. The coming of the railways sapped the whole traffic of the roads, cutting off the flow of travellers who for ages past had journeyed by coach and wagon, horse and foot, and stopped for refreshment at inns large and small. The *Station Hotel*, the *Railway Arms*, and that much-derided institution the station buffet took the custom that used to go to the *Coach and Horses*, the *Wagon and Horses*, the *Jolly Postboys*, the *Packhorse*, and all the other pubs that lived by and off the road. The industrial slums came to

23

(4) By the eighteenth century taverns appeared in political cartoons. (5) At

The

Lamentable Complaints

of

Dick Froth the Tapfter, and Rufcroft the Cooke, concerning the reftraint lately fet forth, againft drinking, potting, and piping on the Sabbath day and againft felling meat.

(Woodcut and extract taken from an old pamphlet printed in 1641).

Cook.—"There is fuch news in the world will anger thee to heare of, it is as bad, as bad may be."

Froth.—"Is there fo ? I pray thee what is it, tell me whatever it be."

Cook.—"Have you not heard of the reftraint lately come out againft us, from the higher powers ; whereby we are commanded not to fell meat nor draw drink upon Sundays, as will anfwer the contrary at our perils." 3

*   *   *   *   *

(3) Legislation appeared at an early date on the question of drink:

8

Flirting

9

Business

from a pass at the pretty tavern wench (8), after Bunbury, 1787, to a business deal—whether in country pub or city coffee house (9).

6

Brawling

7

Sporting

Pub life offered great variety, from a rough house (6), *The Hoigh* Hungerford Market, 1779, to a rest from the chase (7), George Morland, 1788,

create a quite new social environment with its own needs, and the Gin Palace arose to cater for people whose own homes were more wretched than any labourer's cottage. For the first time pubs began to aim at being not only unlike their customers' own homes but unlike anybody's home. In the long drab streets amongst the gas-lights and the railway arches, the pub tried to look unlike any other building that had ever been built. And this development came at the very time when the old slow handicrafts were giving place to the tremendous efflorescence of applied ornament that was glorified in the Great Exhibition of 1851.

The Victorian Gin Palace did not shrink into its squalid surroundings like the tumble-down hovels of Hogarth's *Gin Lane*. It burst out of them with a riot of bow-fronts and engraved glass, and called attention to itself with a gigantic gas lantern, hung on a monster bracket cast in tortured iron. The merest stranger, seeing it from the other end of the street, could not for a second labour under the delusion that it was anything in the world but a pub.

The Gin Palaces were to the Victorian slum what the super-cinemas are to the drab districts today. They brought changes to the traditional forms in which the pub had grown up. With Victorian efficiency the builders planned to increase the turnover; the gin shop was a place designed primarily and obviously for the purpose of selling drink. It did not want to give you a bedroom or a meal, still less did it want to let you wander in, sit down, and talk peacefully to your friends whilst the landlord or his wife roused themselves to come out and see what you would order. You went in and stood at a bar, your order was taken and your drink slapped down. You paid for it, drank it, and had another or went out. The drinking bar was the central point of the planning, and the really efficient town pub had no more use for chairs and tables than a Woolworth's store.

But even efficiency could not overcome the ineradicable class-consciousness of the English, and the undisguised alcoholism of the Victorian pub gave them something to be class-conscious about. So customers had to be segregated from each other whilst still having immediate access to the bar. Hence the intricate and wonderful geography that traced out a dozen different compartments under one rectangular roof, and yet had them all bordered by the same long narrow rivulet of bar. Not just the broad social distinctions of public and private but a proliferation of minor distinctions. We still have our ladies' bars, saloon bars and saloon lounges, wine bars and buffets, each of them sometimes subdivided into two or three, but the gin-shops that Dickens described in the 1830's, during the boom after the Beerhouse Act, rose to such heights of grandiloquence as to have a wine promenade. All these shared the same smoke-stained ceiling, but each had its own partition wall. And to complete the privacy even the bar itself was fenced, in the more select compartments, with wooden frames bearing glass shutters, so that you could slip your order through without looking the barman straight in the face, and feel sure that your indulgence was not being observed from the cheaper compartments where your social inferiors were having one too.

This sort of pub cast a cloak of meanness, depravity, and subterfuge over the business of having a drink. But it did produce a wealth of decoration that is now again admired. With all its faults that was a self-confident age, believing in its own taste and disdaining to hark back to bygone styles. So the teeming interior of the Gin Palace might be full of detail that enchants a connoisseur today. Carvings and mouldings on all the innumerable partitions, intricate decoration dimly seen through the smoke and grime of the ceiling, heavily engraved glass for the windows, the lights in the partitions, the shutters on the bar; bevelled mirrors with drink advertisements gilded in every flourish, in lettering that type-designers have rediscovered since; brass rails, enormous brass pots in which they hardly bothered to put a fern, tiny banisters to every shelf and cupboard-top, every inch of surface carved and fretted down to the mirror-fronted door of the landlord's little cupboard under the stairs: the Gin Palace in its finest form had at least a visual opulence to offset the harm it did.

Of course the nineteenth century did not produce only Gin Palaces, and many of these decorative features are to be found in other types of pub. Many a suburb will still present you with a fine example of the large saloon with leather sofas, rail-topped tables, palms in pots, reproductions of *Derby Day*, and a monumental clock on a massive mantelpiece, as a reminder that the prosperous Victorian pub-goer was not always either quick or furtive in his drinking when he was amongst his equals—and this type of saloon is usually well divided from the public bar. In the late nineteenth century the suburban trains and the omnibuses revived the vogue of the semi-rural pubs whose tea-gardens had been a feature of an earlier age, and some of the seaside houses had an exotic appeal comparable to that of the pier. Catering as they now did for strangers, with no local knowledge to guide them nor post-boys to lead them to the established house, the pubs in all the big centres had every incentive to look like pubs.

But whilst the new pubs were thriving in the towns and the old coaching inns and roadside alehouses were going through a decline, the two great

10

11

national forces that we have summed up briefly as the Nonconformist Conscience and the Brewing Industry were preparing for their biggest battles. The results were to produce most of the odd anomalies that beset the buying and selling of drink in England today.

TWENTIETH CENTURY

Many things in England have changed more in this century than in the seven preceding it, and the public house has borne its share of change. Buffeted by

28

Designed, Etched and Published by GEORGE CRUIKSHANK.]   [November 1st, 1829.

12

13

The craze for gin-drinking marked one of the blackest periods in England's social history, and the gin-shops were being denounced long before the general Victorian reaction against a licentious age set in. Rowlandson's *Dram Shop* (10) from 'The Dance of Death' published in 1815, and Cruikshank's *Blue Ruin* (11) from 'Tom and Jerry', dated 1820, show the gin-shop as a sordid slice of low life in London. As his views grew more serious Cruikshank's caricatures grew harsher and more scathing, until finally, in 1845, he signed the pledge. (12) is taken from his 'Scraps and Sketches', 1829. (13), a drawing of unknown origin, is claimed to be a faithful representation of a Gin Temple near Holborn Hill in the 1830's.

opposing forces—social, political, and economic—the historic pub has performed some strange evolutions since the end of Victoria's reign.

The twentieth century opened with a burst of legislation which did much to change the character of the pubs. The detail of all this legislation is intricate

Mother Louse
of
Louse Hall, near Oxford.
An Alewife at Hedington Hill (1678) mentioned by Anthony Wood.
Probably the last woman in England who wore a ruff.

LOUSE HALL.

14

15

17

18

20

21

30

22 23

The Barmaid (14) An alewife; from a
seventeenth-century woodcut.
(15) An early Victorian barmaid.
(16) A barmaid of the nineties, by
Sir William Nicholson. (17) A contemporary type by Ardizzone.
The Publican (18) Sam House, a well-
known supporter of Charles James
Fox about 1780. The Licensed
Victualler, (19) from an early
nineteenth-century print. (20) An
illustration for 'David Copperfield'
by Phiz. (21) A publican drawn by
Ardizzone.
The Public. The true pub tradition
was preserved in country villages,
where drinking was no more
important than company and conversation. (22) *Drayman and
Coalheaver* by H. Vizetelly from
'Gavarni in London' by
G. S. Chevalier, 1849. (23) *An Inn
Taproom*, by Thomas Silson, *c*. 1840.
(24) A drawing by George du
Maurier of a quiet pub about 1860.

24

and it is not necessary to follow it too closely here.* The Balfour Bill of 1904
provided for reducing the number of licences, which was generally thought
necessary, but introduced the idea of paying compensation for licences sup-

* There are 80 pages of it in the *Brewers' Almanack* for those who want it in full.

25

With the passing of Cruikshank, contemporary artists were again
becoming more interested in the characters found in pubs than in social
reform. Phil May was essentially an observer of London life (25) and
this applies equally to his spiritual successor George Belcher (26).

pressed, with the natural result that whenever one pub in a neighbourhood
was abolished the money value of the surviving licences went up; and then the
Kennedy Judgment of 1906 set the basis of compensation at two or three
times what the government had been prepared to pay. The battle over
compensation was fought furiously in Parliament, and in 1908 the Asquith
Government had a Licensing Bill passed by the Commons and thrown out by
the Lords.

The pub had become an issue in party politics, but by this time the money
value of possessing a licence was an economic factor that could not be ignored.
It is firmly entrenched in the next legal landmark, the Consolidation Act of
1910, which dealt with every issue of compensation, monopoly value, transfer
and removal of licences, plans for new buildings and structural alterations,
closing-times, and such minor matters as off-sales to persons under fourteen
(they were allowed to buy a pint or more at a time in corked or sealed bottles,
thus giving rise to plentiful arguments over what constituted an effective cork

The Lounge at the Warrington

27

The Regulars at the Hero

28

The Public Bar at the George

29

The atmosphere and character of the Victorian pub was never recorded by contemporary artists with the same feeling and understanding that Ardizzone displays in his series of illustrations for Maurice Gorham's 'Back to the Local', (27), (28) and (29). His delightful renderings of engraved glass and carved mahogany, his suggestion of recession charged with mystery in the background, are matched by the superb characterization that he brings to his down-to-earth pub types.

or seal). This Act governed the pubs until the changes brought by the 1914 war, after which the Licensing Act of 1921 created the pubs as most of us have known them, especially with regard to licensing hours.

Another legal change that still affects us was brought in by Lady Astor's Act of 1923 forbidding persons under eighteen to have a drink in a bar; hence the menacing notices that still confront us from so many walls. The effects of the war of 1939 on the pubs were practical rather than legislative, but this war had its sequel in the Licensing Planning Act of 1945, which provided for the removal of licences from bombed districts to new housing areas, and brought in the planning authorities to join the Justices in considering applications. Finally, the Licensing Act of 1949 proposed to establish state management of drinking facilities (first introduced during the 1914 war) in the New Towns.

This is a very short summary of a great deal of legal change, all accompanied by hard debating and widespread controversy. But we must remember that just as parliamentary debates sometimes seem slightly remote from reality, so parliamentary enactments do not always give a good guide to subsequent behaviour. For instance, ever since the Licensing Act of 1921 there have been no legal closing-times for pubs; there are only 'permitted hours' during which the publican can lawfully sell alcoholic drinks. But no casual customer threatened by the cry of 'Time, gentlemen, please' has the hardihood to say he will stay on and have a nice cup of tea or a small dry ginger, and it is easy to imagine what would happen if he did.

The real point is how far all this legislation reflected and how far it affected the drinking habits of the people and the places where they drank. By the beginning of the century the pub was already very different from the ale-houses and inns from which it sprang. Road travel, killed by the railways, had not yet been revived by the motor-car, and the old mixed trade in wine, spirits, beer, meals, beds, and horses had become mainly a straightforward trade in spirits and beer. Draught beer gives the publican his closest link with his supplier. He can get his bottled goods by mail order if he likes but for his draught beer he must be in close physical touch with the brewery. He has to organize his cellar space and times of drawing, and if his beer does not come when he expects it his trade will suffer a mortal blow.

The brewery on its side has a lively interest in the way its draught beer is kept and served, apart from its natural desire to have it sold in as many houses as possible, and best of all to have it on sale without competition from any other brewer's beer. So the brewing industry became the greatest owner of public houses. Brewers used their profits on the sale of beer to buy up pubs and

34

to build new pubs, sometimes putting in a salaried manager but most often letting them to individual tenants whose application for a licence they backed and who in return took all their draught beer, and sometimes other products as well, from the brewery that owned the house.

This tied-house system has been the source of much embittered controversy, especially since the big breweries began to serve large areas and own great numbers of pubs. There is plenty to be said both for and against the system, and it is constantly being said. So far as we are concerned here, its chief effect is to put big money behind the individual pub, to make it part of a well-organized concern whose interest is primarily in selling a certain kind of beer, and to bring it under some measure of central control.

Such a pub may have grown up with the locality but it no longer derives purely from its surroundings. It belongs to a business that can afford to retain leading lawyers to defend its licence, and to alter it, rebuild it, even abolish it, in the overall interests of the brewery. It is aimed by experts at a target, and the target is primarily the sale of one brewery's beer.

The tied-house system arose quite naturally, but there have been attempts to devise alternatives to it. The public house trusts, for instance, set out to buy up chains of pubs, as the brewers do, but to make them into genuine refreshment houses and sever the publican from any interest in the sale of drink. The State Management Scheme, introduced during the 1914–18 war and put on a peace-time footing by the Licensing Act of 1921, gave the State a monopoly of the drink business in certain limited areas, notably Carlisle. The majority of the Royal Commission on Licensing in England and Wales that reported in 1932 approved of this scheme and recommended that it should be given a wider trial in rather different conditions, with less centralized state control. This is the system that the Licensing Act of 1949 proposes to apply to the New Towns.

Meanwhile the workings of redundancy and compensation had been sweeping away the old pubs. After the Act of 1904 the demolition of old houses went on apace, aided by the fact that many licensing Justices had got no further in their study of the drink question than a belief that it is better to have one pub than two or three, and beamed on any proposal to demolish a pub.

Proposals to modernize pubs rather than to demolish them have had a mixed reception according to the composition of the local Bench. Some reformers sternly oppose any improvements that might make pubs more attractive, and especially any addition to the space on which you can sell

(30) Main Bar and plan of *The College Arms*, Birmingham, designed by Harrison and Cox and built in 1913.

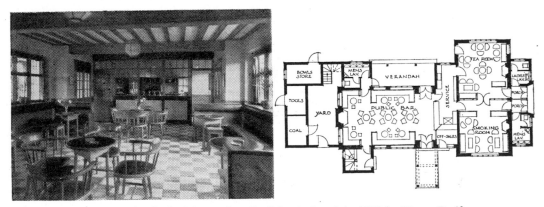

(31) Public Bar and plan of *The Magpie Inn*, Carlisle, designed in 1933 by Harry Redfern.

The illustrations on this and the facing page show the break with tradition which occurred during the first half of this century. (See also pages 115–120.)

The 'improved public house' originated in Birmingham in 1897 with the Birmingham 'surrender' scheme. Certain licences were transferred from crowded central areas to new houses in the suburbs. This was made possible by co-operation between the brewers and the licensing Justices. The new pubs were notable for the re-introduction of long bars and for the elimination of sub-divisions.

The Carlisle undertaking was set up in 1916 to acquire all breweries and pubs in an area covering 500 square miles. Early reforms aimed mainly at remodelling existing houses. 'Snugs' gave way to

(32) Plan and Saloon Bar of *The Cherry Tree*, Welwyn Garden City, Herts, designed in 1933 by R. G. Muir.

(33) Plan and Public Lounge of *The Downham Tavern*, Downham, Kent.

open bars, customers were encouraged to sit at tables rather than stand at the bar. The bar-counter became little more than a service hatch.

The Welwyn scheme, sponsored jointly by the Welwyn Garden City Company and Whitbread's, introduced a new conception; the pub should not only serve food and drink, but act as a community centre for all the activities that go to make a full family life in an urban community.

The Downham Tavern, the largest pub ever built, was designed in 1930 for a large L.C.C. estate. Over half of it was a theatre where the public could watch the show and drink beer at the same time.

drink. Others welcome any move to heighten the family atmosphere and take the emphasis off the sale of drink, so they approve of dining-rooms and lounges and tea gardens and anything that makes the pub, in the eyes of some of its older habitués, less like a pub.

The second point of view has prevailed and the 'improved public house' has gradually won its way. Who is responsible for it is a matter of dispute; credit has been given to the trust companies, to State Management, and to the tied-house system. But coupled with the wave of demolition, it has wrought great changes in the appearance and character of the English pub.

The pubs have always been undergoing alteration and demolition, and every antiquary's researches read like a casualty list, but the process can never have been so drastic and so deliberate as it has been in this century. It went on most merrily between the wars, and this was perhaps unfortunate, for whatever can be said for the general level of invention and craftsmanship, there was certainly little of the feeling that had stamped the best of the old pubs. And the 'improved public house' is likely to last for a long time, but the styles of the twenties and thirties do not always age well.

The war of 1939 was the next blow to the pubs: the bombing was as drastic as the pre-war demolitions and even less planned. To the pub-goer it seemed as though the pubs had more than their share of hits, perhaps because so many of them stand on corner sites and are more exposed to blast. Naturally the older pubs were the more vulnerable, and many a quiet old house in a back street or up the alley collapsed into a heap of rubble, leaving behind no relics except perhaps that most durable of fittings, the tiled wall of the 'Gents'. Some of the oldest parts of our cities now form a veritable graveyard of little neighbourhood pubs.

In 1942 the government appointed a committee to consider the effects of the war on the pubs, and the result was the Morris Report of 1944, which laid down the creed of the 'improved public house' and confirmed the trends towards replacement of several small pubs by one bigger one, provision of tables and chairs indoors and gardens and bowling-greens outside, even if this meant enlarging the premises, and the supply of food both in dining-rooms and in the bars; but it did put in a good word for the smaller pub.

Since the war the rebuilding of old pubs has been at a standstill, but the Morris Report has set the pattern for the new houses. This is the type of house that the Licensing Planning authorities will most easily approve for the new housing areas, and it will be this type of house that we can expect to find being built under the new Licensing Act in the New Towns.

In the traditional Victorian Gin Palace (34), the equipment was exploited as an essential part of its decoration. Its space was divided into small bars, originally to separate the social classes, but these also provided semi-seclusion for small groups in the middle of a crowd, as for instance in (35), the Private Bar.

This Act, of course, caused all the controversies to flare up again in their angriest form, but from the point of view of what the pubs will be like it does not seem to make very much difference whether the government builds them or the brewers. Whatever their motives, they are not far divided in their ideas as to what constitutes the improved modern pub. Both employ expert architects and designers, both go in for refined exteriors and well-planned interiors with plenty of light and air and, in most cases, modern materials used in a modern way. There is little to choose visually between the new pubs of Park Royal and the new pubs of Carlisle. But to the eye of the traditionalist, none of them look particularly like pubs.

THE PEOPLE IN THE PUBS

This brief retrospect of the legal and social factors that have shaped the growth of the English public house necessarily gives a one-sided view of the pubs themselves. Brewers and architects can plan pubs, Parliament and the

Bench can control them, but the pub as a living institution depends on the sort of people who find their way into it, on both sides of the bar.

If it is dangerous to generalize about the pubs of the past on the evidence that we have about them, it is even more dangerous to generalize about the people who went to them. The illustrations of pub interiors reproduced here give a lot of guidance, but before deducing too much from them you have to consider how difficult it would be to illustrate all the types and variety of pub interiors and pub-goers even today. The same pub may have totally different *clientèles* at lunch-time and in the evening, and a pub that you have known as a crowded bustling drinking-shop with the cash-register ringing continuously may turn at week-ends into a quiet resort where a few regulars gossip intermittently over their well-spaced drinks.

Even period seems to waver in the pubs. In modern houses you naturally expect to find modern people, dressed in the standardized fashions of the multiple stores, but in many pubs near the river, the markets, and the warehouses, where men go in their working clothes, you might think you had slipped back into the nineteenth century. And in some wine-houses and cider-stores the customers look as though they came from a different world from that of the milk bars and the cinema queues.

All one can say is that the people who go to the pubs have changed as the people of England changed, though not always at quite the same rate. Modern pub-goers are quieter than they used to be, more respectable, less apt to quarrel and much less apt to fight; but so are people everywhere. Unescorted young women of the respectable sort go to pubs now more than they used to, but so do they go to theatres and restaurants and speedway tracks. The greatest change, perhaps, is that many people, both men and women, now lunch in the pubs near their business premises without having even one drink. In this generation the pubs have probably widened further than ever their appeal to all classes and all ages, with the single exception of the under-eighteens, whom the law allows to drink in a restaurant but not in a bar.

Pubs are made by the people who go to them, but there are many factors that cause different sorts of people to go to different sorts of pubs: food, drink, games, company, neighbourhood, and of course the personality of the landlord and his staff. But the building itself is a factor too. There are some pub interiors that feel sociable even if you are the only person in the bar, and some that never feel sociable even when they are packed to the doors. It is here that the brewers and the architects can give a pub a good start, and they

40

(36) The Wine Bar, a specialized type with its own clientèle, often with a business or sporting background, depended to a remarkable degree on the arrangement of barrels for its major architectural effect, and in this is even more a direct heir of the gin shop (No. 10) than the Victorian pub.

37

can make their own task easier if they remember that the English pub is a traditional institution, and there is a lot of experience to draw upon apart from the brave new ideas that have sprung up since 1914.

(37) The Kitchen, the original from which the pub developed, is still to be found throughout the country, sometimes very little changed despite 200 years of progress.

THE TRADITION *by* H. McG. Dunnett

The habits, needs and preferences of the people who use pubs, described in the preceding pages, can now be translated into architectural—that is to say visual—terms. The evolution of the pub tradition is traced from the days when it was little more than the kitchen of a wayside cottage, to the highly specialized interior of the last century with its characteristic fittings and decorations—and beyond. Special attention is paid to that period piece the Victorian Gin Palace, in its own way a work of art. But behind it lies the much older pub tradition, to be found in every village and country town; of casks, settles, scrubbed tables, a bit of brass, good lettering, an Act of Parliament clock, china rum and whisky barrels behind the bar and a brilliantly varnished ceiling. This very real tradition wants safeguarding and continuing.

BEGINNINGS

The English pub has been a part of the English landscape for centuries. For this very reason there are unlimited examples of pub exteriors—wayside pubs, street scene pubs, pubs with queer signs, famous pubs and infamous, quite apart from the vast literature available on inns, but the interior of the pub *per se* has, in contrast, been almost neglected. Contemporary illustrators and writers who have dealt with the pub, tavern, or alehouse scene have been interested mainly with the characters found there and with their many and varied activities, but even these records are few and widely scattered.

Although every pub was different there is, fortunately, a homogeneity due on the one hand to the common aspects of the trade which they plied and on the other, at least before the nineteenth century, to the limitations of building techniques. Even that century's developments are to a large extent stereotyped throughout the country, because the publicans who built them and the architects who designed them were by then sufficiently mobile to find out what their rivals were doing.

In the towns they followed town domestic architecture, until the 'Gin Palace' of the early nineteenth century introduced a new, almost theatrical, break with this tradition. But from the sixteenth century to the eighteenth pub interiors must have changed little and many continued unchanged till well into the next century, particularly in rural areas.

'Home from Home' is therefore a useful pub classification which speaks

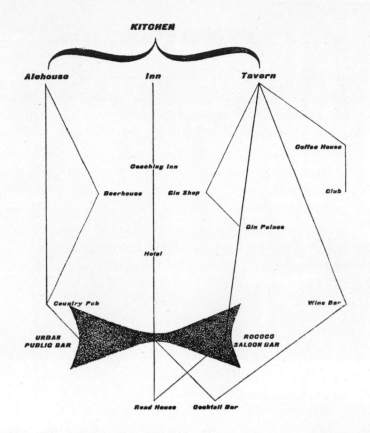

(38) **The Evolution of Pub Types.** The story begins, centuries ago, in any wayside house that
opened its kitchen for the sale of drinks to passers by. Its architectural ambitions were merely to be
a home from home. But soon three types clearly distinguished themselves: the simple alehouse, the
inn (which provided beds as well as food and drink), and the tavern which satisfied the more
sophisticated demand of the town customer for wine as well as beer. From the alehouse sprang the
simple beerhouse of the country village or town by-street, and from its simple forms derived the
architectural character both of the typical country pub and the Public Bar in the big town pub. The
inn grew to be a good deal grander than home, became the coaching inn, passed beyond the pub
category as the railway hotel, but reappeared as the flashy road house of the motor-car era. The
hotel also produced the modern Cocktail Bar. The tavern developed into the coffee house, and
thence into the club; secondly into the Wine Bar, which was also partly responsible for the Cocktail
Bar; and thirdly into the highly specialized pub interior that we find today at the street corner in
every town. By way of the gin shop it became the Gin Palace, creating that specialist kind
of interior decoration, with a frankly theatrical appeal, that had little in common with domestic
interior decoration. This style is seen at its best in the rococo Saloon Bar of the town pub, where it
pairs up again with the more simply styled Public Bar, whose architectural descent is here
separately traced almost direct from the alehouse kitchen.

40

39

The Alehouse or 'Home from Home' Tradition. This is the main stem of the family tree, represented here by a typical Rowlandson sketch of an alehouse kitchen (39) and its present-day urban counterpart, the Public Bar, in this case *The Anchor* at Bankside (40). This is the kitchen tradition from which the next two types emerged, and it must be the starting-point for any new pub development.

for itself and represents a continuing tradition which is still widespread and still eminently satisfactory.

The other two classifications both refer to the nineteenth century. The 'Grander than Home' is a type which is fairly common in oldish suburbs and small towns. It is very nearly a hotel sometimes and may even have passed through and out of that stage. It might even have been an inn but just missed the coach. On the other hand it approaches close to the Victorian pub but is a

46

41

The Inn or 'Grander than Home' Tradition. The interior of *The Queen's Head*, at Islington in 1840, (42), provides the key to the second tradition. Starting from the kitchen it has become the coaching inn; despite the simple wall benches and furniture it seeks consciously to impress with its scale and mural ornamentation. Its Victorian counterpart (41), *The Woodman* Birmingham, achieves the same formal pompous grandeur.

42

shade too aware of being 'Grander than Home' to make it a comfortable pub for the average pub-goer.

The third is the 'Frankly Theatrical', the Victorian pub that glorified in its self-advertisement. It is sometimes called a Gin Palace, a term which is more an endearment today than the reproach that it used to be. It appears too that these underwent considerable changes throughout the century, and the Victorian rococo pub which we see today is a very respectable old lady

44

The Tavern or 'Frankly Theatrical' Tradition. The Gin Palace burst on the urban scene in 1830 and converted the tavern, from its kitchen and gin shop beginnings, into a display of dazzling showmanship, as shown by Cruikshank (43). Out of this tradition emerged the remarkable functional and decorative qualities of the Victorian Gin Palace, apparent in (44), the Saloon Bar of *The Unicorn*, Shoreditch.

43

compared with what she was in her dashing 'teens of the '30's and '40's.

In keeping to pubs, an effort has been made to avoid coaching inns, coffee houses and the historical show-places, except where illustrations of these have been valuable to emphasize a particular point or relationship with pub tradition. The first of these is of course already well documented and in any case catered primarily for travellers. The second, likewise a special subject, was for a time a kind of better class tavern but, by the mid-eighteenth century, custom was changing them into either eating-houses or clubs. As for the show-places, these tend to emphasize particular oddities rather than a tradition and sometimes the traditional features have been too clearly added or replaced for them to be reliable guides.

Who designed the pubs? Before the nineteenth century history does not relate. Architects were designing pubs by the 1830's, but the names do not convey much. Loudon's *Cyclopædia of Cottage, Farm and Villa Architecture* gives designs for a 'small Village Inn, or Alehouse in the Italian Gothic manner' by M. E. Hadfield of Doncaster, a Mr. Laxton 'who has had great experience in fitting up public houses' designed a 'Suburban Public House in the old English style' and to 'Mr. John Robertson, architect of Bayswater, near London' Loudon is indebted for a 'small Inn or Public House in the Swiss style.' Mr. Kempshott, a London architect, he mentions as having 'built numerous public houses and also some country churches and one or two mausoleums.' Stephen Geary is alleged elsewhere to have designed the first Gin Palace, his only other claims to fame as far as we can discover being a stucco monument at King's Cross, heartily condemned by Pugin, and Highgate Cemetery.

From the 1860's on, certain names like E. L. Paraire, Edle and Meyers and B. J. Capell crop up frequently and when the brewers became responsible for building pubs they continued to employ practising architects. It was not till the rapid development after 1918 that in many cases they set up their own architects' departments and that really prominent architects turned their attentions to the design of pubs. What they made of them is considered further on. What the future holds for the pub is the purpose of this book.

THE RURAL TRADITION

The 'Home from Home' pub was the country pub with no pretensions but plenty of homely frills. In its true form still to be found all over the country today, even in London and other big cities, it is the eighteenth-century tradition by-passed almost completely by the urban tradition of the nineteenth.

It has no particular plan, it has just grown from the days when the kitchen was the main room—not the best room but always the warmest.

There are many variations but even when an enterprising publican has, in the later nineteenth century, fitted a solid mahogany bar-top or even introduced a mahogany bar fitment, the country pub element is still unmistakable in the irregularities of its arrangement.

The pub of country origin which we know today developed from the kitchen by way of the tap-room to the public bar. Old records show the kitchen as the operative room prior to the nineteenth century, with its rough interior, solid settles and large fireplace with all the necessary cooking paraphernalia of the hearth. Above the fireplace, shelves and racks loaded with polished pewter and copperware or saucepan lids are the only other decorative features of the room.

In the towns they were frequently more elaborate, corresponding to their higher standards of decoration, using panelled walls, large ornately carved fireplaces and plaster ceilings in high relief, and it is apparent that the kitchen as a cooking room was, by the end of the eighteenth century, withdrawing from the room occupied by the customers, though probably the lower order of customer retired with it.

This feature of the kitchen continued well into the last century, at least in rural areas, for new ideas spread slowly and it was probably not till the urban pub established the idea of separate bars linked by a bar-counter that the kitchen became a tap-room and later a public bar, or that bar-counters appeared in country pubs at all.

The bar-counter, which is discussed in detail later on, did not become a popular feature till the nineteenth century. Its function was to help the staff to maintain control and to stop the customers from helping themselves. When it was established it was usually of oak, as this does not warp or split easily, though ash was also used, and probably elm and chestnut, the indigenous woods preferred for a solid job of that sort by generations of country carpenters. In shipbuilding towns and ports, where foreign woods were more readily obtainable, these were used too; in fact Liverpool has many examples of teak bar-counters. The vertical front of the counter was generally from boards of the same wood as the top, or of softer woods such as pitch pine, which served the purpose just as well. The architect of the suburban pub illustrated on page 66, however, insists on mahogany for his bar-counter.

In rural areas the wood surfaces were probably untreated oak, the tops of the bar-counter and tables assuming a pleasing natural polish from the daily spillings of ale, still held by many today who should know, to be the finest polish of all. The benches and high-backed fireside seats certainly received their share of burnishing from generations of rustic hindquarters.

Furniture in both country and town pubs was very limited, in fact the illustrations which show rooms with no occupants are practically bare, apart from a table, a bench and two or three chairs.

Floors in country pubs were of stone flags, bricks and sometimes boards, while walls and ceilings were of plain or whitewashed plaster, the matchboard-

(45) The early pub was no whit different from the ordinary dwelling or farmhouse. The public room was the kitchen with its open hearth and simple equipment. The alehouse kitchen by George Morland, 1788, shows this primitive form, little more than a modest domestic room in a rural cottage.

(46) This alehouse kitchen scene by Rowlandson, dated about 1810, is similar to one in his 'Dr Syntax' series. In it the kitchen begins to take the shape of a country pub. The partitioned structure in the corner is the taproom where the day's supply of ale, brought from the nearby brewhouse, is stored, and where the serving wenches replenish their pitchers. The familiar high-backed settle is there and so is the typical decorative element above the mantelshelf.

(47) *Parties in a Tavern Kitchin* is the title of this scene. Though it predates the two previous illustrations by a century and is almost certainly urban rather than rural, the same basic elements are apparent, particularly the typical equipment of hearth and overmantel. The use of carefully stowed kitchen utensils as unconscious decoration reappears later in the pub as the tradition by which barrels, bottles and containers serve the same functional but decorative purpose behind the bar-counter.

ing seen today probably appearing considerably later in the nineteenth century.

All pubs, however, being normal domestic dwellings, had the usual private quarters for the proprietor and in particular the parlour. This was the private room to which guests were taken if they did not wish to mix socially with the lower orders in the kitchen. It was equipped with the publican's best furniture and probably boasted a table, any upholstery he had managed to acquire—there was little available to the poorer classes of the eighteenth century—a dresser and a collection of his most prized personal odds and ends. These would reflect his interest in some sport or pursuit, perhaps earlier days spent in foreign parts and probably a small collection of family heirlooms. During the nineteenth century this collection was undoubtedly expanded with a wealth of stuffed fish, birds and animals, trinkets, souvenirs and antimacassars.

These parlours still exist today, particularly in the north where, often, the bar-counter does not extend outside the public bar. Where conditions changed, it became the private bar, subsequently fading away when the saloon bar pushed it into the background.

Colour in the 'Home from Home' pub has always stemmed from home-grown woods, particularly oak in its natural state. Paintwork, and particularly graining, has always followed this tradition of natural oak, though the popularity of mahogany during the nineteenth century led to the use of this wood and its grained imitation too, and the same applied to teak. Walls have tended to keep to wood or plaster colours even when papered, decorated papers being more common in the parlour when that room has retained its identity. Decoration really owes more to the incidental additions of the publican himself, some pubs being veritable museums of traditional ale pots in pewter and glazed slipware, and ranges of spirit measures in pewter and copper which have outlived their usefulness and often their accuracy. Floral decoration rarely goes beyond ferns and the evergreen plants that seem to live in pots for ever. In latter days, however, the advertising efforts of the brewers, distillers and the soft drink, tobacco and potato crisp manufacturers have provided unlimited supplies of enamelled and cardboard wall placards, china jugs, dogs and brisk-stepping gentlemen in fancy dress, and any pub nowadays would look barren indeed without its quota of advertising bric-à-brac.

The resulting colours, furniture and lighting all merge unobtrusively, as if by instinct, to form a quiet background to the people for whom the pub exists.

THE ORIGINS OF THE BAR-COUNTER

When the bar-counter originated is not clear. The Oxford Dictionary says that a bar is mentioned in Greene's *Art of Conny Catching* dated 1592, but it is quite clear that that was not a bar-counter as we know it. The bar-counter almost certainly developed first in the coffee house, that is, it had an urban origin. It is also very probable that a form of bar developed independently in the kitchen of the country alehouse and for rather different reasons, but ultimately the two knit together to become a single line of development sometime in the mid-nineteenth century.

The early alehouse kitchen had no pub characteristics and was no more than the humble domestic farmhouse kitchen depicted in the George Morland alehouse scene on page 51. The brewhouse was across the yard at the back and whenever a fresh supply of ale was required, someone had to go out with a pitcher and draw it off. This naturally became rather inconvenient when there was, perhaps, a friendly invasion by the military and business was brisk, and particularly so when the yard was dark, dirty and muddy. The

Servery into Bar-back. The Tap-room was originally a servery-cum-store, the halfway point between the brewhouse across the yard and the customers in the kitchen. From this beginning the kitchen pub developed its own bar, as the partitioned-off sanctum was the natural place to store containers, drinking vessels and the equipment needed to serve the drink. When the upper part of the partition disappeared and the bar-counter was fitted across the front, the containers and other apparatus were ranged across the back, as this was the most convenient position for serving. (48), the servery in *The George*, South-wark, is compared with the ordered array of bottles and casks in (49), *Geare's Wine Bar*, Marylebone, which is its direct descendant.

(50) *The Beehive* at Hatfield Hyde in Hertfordshire, not twenty-five miles from London, has a Public Bar which is a perfect example of the traditional alehouse. Simple, factual and unadorned, it is not far departed from the farmhouse kitchen. The stone flags are only part-hidden by a modern floor covering, and the solid half door is not far removed from the barn. But the built-in wooden bench, with its curved seat and the flowing shapely end to the high back, is pure pub tradition; its influence can be seen in pubs

56

that have reached a much more developed stage. (51) (*above*) The Public Bar in *The Waggoners*, another Hertfordshire pub, suggests that the process of domestication has gone a stage or two further than that of *The Beehive* opposite. The effect is still one of solid simple furnishings but the tradition of painted wood boards in wood colours is representative of the pub's decorative vernacular.

52

The Inglenook becomes a Room. The kitchen has always revolved round the fireplace. When the pub evolved from the kitchen, it took over the idea of a pleasant nook or alcove, where draughts and cold could be excluded, and where the elders could enjoy their ale, pipes and conversation in peaceful seclusion. As the kitchen function disappeared, this element quite naturally expanded to take over the whole room. (52) *An Alehouse Kitchen* by Morland *c.* 1790. (53) *The Mill Inn*, Witherington, Gloucestershire. (54) The existing chimney corner in *The George*, Southwark.

53

54

The Bar-Counter is a town tradition. It probably started as the queer contraption, shown in (55), that looks like a four-poster. The scene is a seventeenth-century coffee house in Paris and the grand lady, probably of the race of 'Limonadière,' controls the dispensing of liquor, pipes and tobacco.

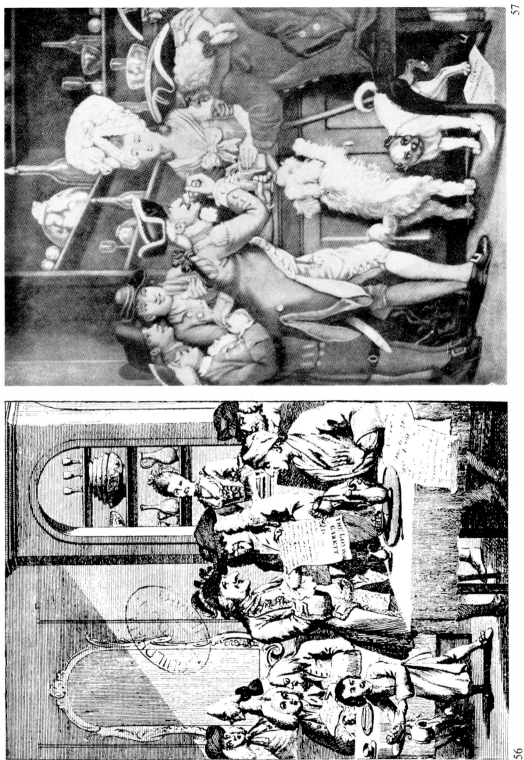

57

56

By the eighteenth century the English tradition had evolved the Georgian 'niche' (56), and in this coffee house scene its soft curve is adapted to the handy storage and service of cordials and spirits. In the course of time convenience demanded more space behind the bar-counter, while the happy combination of an attractive barmaid and a counter to lean on are not lost on the customers, as (57) shows; this is from a painting by John Collet, c.1750.

(58) By the early nineteenth century the bar-counter had grown yet bigger due to the habit of perpendicular drinking, and was acquiring its specialized equipment. In the place of the niche appeared the first signs of the decorated Victorian bar-back.

obvious thing to do was to provide a room or cubby-hole inside the house where a bulk supply could be stored, sufficient at least for the requirements of one evening. So in a corner of the kitchen, a little area was partitioned off and turned into a store. This is illustrated very clearly in Rowlandson's drawing on page 52, where it is conveniently placed by the back door, equipped with a hatch and somewhat withdrawn from the populated part of the room. It is occupied—and guarded—by a responsible older woman, probably the proprietor's wife and there the serving wenches replenish their pitchers. This was undoubtedly the origin of the alehouse tap-room. Such a room may have existed outside the actual public room, but it is its situation within it that is of particular interest here, for it only needs the upper part of the partitioning to be removed and a table to be stood in front, or better still a shelf put round it, to make it ideal as a servery as well as a store. The diagrams on pages 64–5 show how the tap-room, in its original pub sense, was sacrosanct to the proprietor and staff. As the kitchen lost its identity as a place for cooking, the name 'tap-room' passed to the public room and the private part was called the 'bar'. Later the same fate overtook the bar. In course of time the names for the different rooms that were taken over by the public changed several times under the influence of urban usage. In due course the bar-counter was moved into the centre of the room on the urban model, and quite logically, for there it was more conveniently placed to serve all the rooms.

The evidence suggests, however, that in the country, the bar as we know it did not appear generally till Victorian times. There is certainly not much information to go on, but Loudon's *Cyclopædia of Cottage, Farm and Villa Architecture*, published in 1833 and referred to earlier, gives a number of architects' plans for public houses of various sizes and not one makes provision in a country pub for a bar-counter as we know it. Where a bar is shown, it is the publican's private room. The room for the general public, apart from the parlour, is the tap-room. Since no supplies are stored in that room, it shows that already the name had changed its meaning. A selection of these plans are given on pages 66–7, and it will be seen that the design for a suburban public house does have a bar and bar-counter, in fact a very involved bar-counter. The reason for this bar-counter, to quote from the description accompanying the plan, is that liquor is 'either drank in the shop, standing at the counter, or carried home in brought vessels by the purchasers'. This is of course the urban influence, for bar-counters were by then standard in gin shops and probably in other forms of urban pubs.

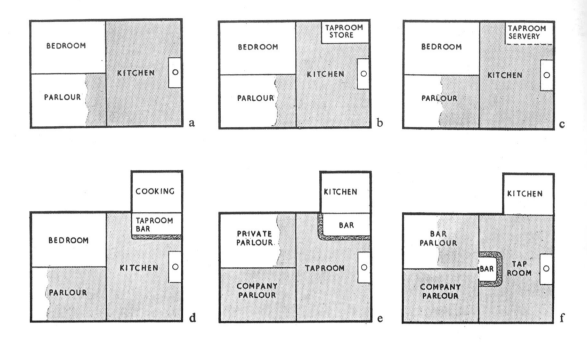

The urban form of the bar-counter came about in a different way, and, as mentioned earlier, almost certainly originated in the coffee house. An illustration (page 60) dating from about 1700, of a scene in what is probably a Parisian coffee house, shows a contraption half-way between a four-poster bed frame and a cashier's desk, which looks very like the beginnings of a bar and bar-counter. It is occupied by a female rather like a high priestess but who actually is *la belle Limonadière*, a member of a very select guild of lemonade dispensers. She sits there to dispense the liquor, pipes and tobacco, and presumably also looks after the money. The English domestic influence wrought a subtle change, which is apparent in the illustration of an eighteenth-century London coffee house (page 61), for the Georgian 'niche' has been adapted with shelves behind for crockery and a small counter in front for serving. Here is the bar-counter, and in fact the Victorian bar-back, in embryo. The lady behind the counter, too, is not the alarming looking character in the French edition.

This process continues, the Georgian 'niche' is expanded for greater convenience and better storage and in John Collet's painting of *The Pretty Barmaid*, page 61, the situation becomes more complex, for the happy combination of an attractive barmaid and a substantial counter to lean on is

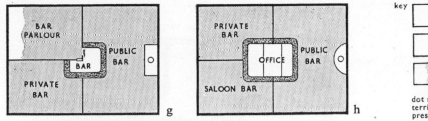

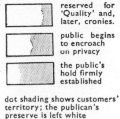

(59) **The Bar takes over the House.** *These diagrams illustrate the progress from kitchen to pub, how the country pub used the bar, and how the names of the bars evolved.* **a,** the original pub had one public room, the kitchen. Ale was fetched as required from the brewhouse and the owner's Parlour was available should 'The Quality' arrive; the back room was the family bedroom. It was George Morland's alehouse kitchen (45), page 51. **b,** later a store or Taproom was partitioned off in the kitchen to obviate frequent trips to the brewhouse, as in the Rowlandson drawing (46), page 52. In **c** a hatch is let into the Taproom partition to permit service direct. **d,** a counter to stand the pots on, is added across the hatch. For convenience the cooking room is moved, though the name 'kitchen' lingers. The Parlour is losing its privacy. **e,** the Kitchen becomes the Taproom, taking the name of the corner room, now called the Bar, having a counter on two sides. The Parlour, now fully occupied, becomes the Company Parlour. and the bedroom makes way for the publican's Private Parlour. **f,** the corner Bar is scrapped, and a new one built in the middle of the Taproom, with a hatch to the Company Parlour and a curtain to the Private Parlour, now renamed Bar Parlour. **g,** the kitchen vanishes. The names establish the invaders' success; the term 'Bar' is applied to all the customers' territory. The Taproom becomes the Public Bar, and the Company Parlour is now the Private Bar, with the counter extended through; the invasion of the Bar Parlour proceeds. In the last scene, **h,** the Bar Parlour becomes the Private Bar; the front room is renamed Saloon Bar to accord with urban custom; the publican is left with an office only, now surrounded completely by the bar-counter.

not lost on the customers, nor on the proprietor, in all probability. It heralds the nineteenth-century habit of perpendicular drinking around which the whole of bar design has since evolved.

By the early nineteenth century, the urban bar-counter had grown yet bigger to deal with the greater traffic of the towns, and was beginning to acquire its specialized equipment. Cruikshank's gin-shop scene, *Life in the East*, on page 62, one of the famous *Tom and Jerry* series, shows a 'fountain' or cordial dispenser on the counter, just beyond the two ducks in the basket. The counter itself is much bigger, while the 'niche' has vanished completely and in its place is the formal forerunner of the decorated Victorian bar-back with casks, bottles and glasses thoughtfully arranged to be decorative as well as handy.

The use in this way of the essential equipment of the pub as decoration became traditional and it is apparent not only in the gin shop and early Gin Palace, but today in the Victorian pub and even more strongly in the wine

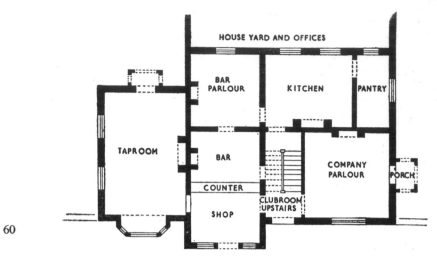

60

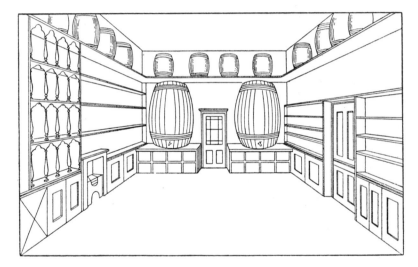

61

62

66

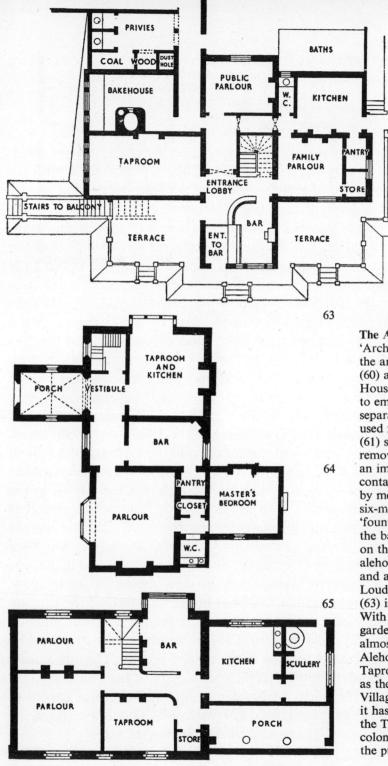

63

64

65

67

The Architect Takes over. Loudon's 'Architecture' reveals the influence of the architect on pubs as early as 1833. (60) a plan for a 'Suburban Public House' is the only design in the book to employ a bar-counter, which here separates the 'bar' from the 'shop' used for the 'bottle and jug' trade. (61) shows the 'bar' with the counter removed, its shelves designed to make an impressive display of casks and containers. These casks are connected by means of pipes either with the six-motion beer-engine or with the 'fountain' or spirit dispenser built into the bar-counter (62). The three plans on this page are intended to show alehouses and inns of different sizes, and are also reproduced from Loudon's 'Architecture'. (63) is a 'Small Inn or Public House'. With a Family Parlour, terraces and gardens and a clubroom upstairs it is almost a family pub. (64) is a 'Hedge Alehouse of the Smallest Size', the Taproom and Kitchen still combined as the main public room. (65) a 'Small Village Inn or Alehouse', is unusual as it has two Parlours, both bigger than the Taproom, and a pleasant colonnaded Porch. In each the 'bar' is the publican's private domain.

bar. It is, moreover, a tradition that comes directly from the kitchen where the polished pewter and copperware filled the racks about the fireplace in orderly splendour.

THE EARLY GIN PALACE

It is always convenient to chop history up into centuries and the nineteenth century lends itself very well to this treatment. In comparison with the past the changes were very rapid and far-reaching, and the effect they had on the pub reflected the achievements and the shortcomings of the times.

A philosophy of individualism and materialism, coupled with an enormous outburst of technical invention, caused the greatest shift of population in the country's history, as the manufacturing towns sucked the population off the land into their congested urban growth. This process has continued ever since. The village pubs remained much as they were, unless, overtaken by the expanding towns, they were swept away in the fury of the changing order. Many, however, managed to weather the storm and can be found to this day much as they might have been in 1800. In the new towns thousands of pubs sprang up where there were none before, and they assumed new shapes and guises which bore little resemblance to what had existed before.

Like all English institutions, the English pub has assimilated changing customs and tastes. The flamboyant Gin Palace of the 1830's described below heralded the maturer plan of the Victorian urban pub which marked a violent break with the tradition of the alehouse kitchen, both in style of decoration and in its conscious planning. A new plan for the pub was inevitable, as the old model had no means of coping with urban crowds. The new appearance resulted from the new conditions of competition. The joint solution was, in the circumstances, a logical one, and certainly the Victorian plan has been the model for all pubs designed since. As the war has brought a halt to conscious demolition it is worth taking stock of them before it starts anew.

To reconstruct the changes that came about in the first half of the century one must reconstruct the history of drink. The drink problem was so much in the forefront of politics and social reform that few writers or illustrators who dealt with pubs can be trusted to give an unbiased record. George Cruikshank, for instance, one of the most prolific chroniclers of the contemporary scene, turned teetotal in the midst of his career and the cheerful capers of *Tom and Jerry* were replaced even by 1829 with *The Gin Shop*, page 29, followed by *The Drunkard's Children* and other cautionary tales.

The biggest hiatus is the period 1830 to 1870, as the evidence is meagre,

Oh tell us Sir Andrew, whose puritan zeal
To Sabbath profaners destruction shall
   deal.
Did you ever behold such a sample of sin
As a church time turn-out from a
   Temple of Gin?
Costermongers, coal heavers, dustmen
   and drabs,
Swell omnibus jarveys and drivers of cabs,
The bell chimes to church and out
   stagger the queer 'uns,
from Wellers in Old Street and
   Thompsons and Fearons.

Gin-temple turn-out at Church time.

(66) The illustration comes from 'Sunday in London' by George Cruikshank

conflicting and confusing. We know pretty well what rococo Victorian pubs looked like from 1870 onwards, because we can see them today. What we do not know is whether the earlier ones were similar or different. Cruikshank shows his *Tom and Jerry* in 1821 in a gin-shop with the beginnings of a flashy rococo Victorian pub. By the time he reaches his temperance series his Gin Palaces have become florid in an eighteenth-century manner. In 1833 Cruikshank writes: 'In the grey of the Sunday morning, at the sound of the matin bell, the gin temples open wide their portals to all comers. Time was when gin was to be found only in bye-lanes and blind alleys—in dirty, obscure holes, y'clep'd dram shops, but now, thanks to the enlightened and paternal government of "the first captain of the age" gin is become a great demi-god, a mighty spirit dwelling in gaudy gold-be-plastered temples.' He then goes on to quote a contemporary: 'The expense incurred in the fitting up of gin-shop bars in London is almost incredible, everyone vying with his neighbour in convenient arrangements, general display, rich carving, brass-work, finely veined mahogany, gilding and ornamental painting. The carving of one ornament alone in the Grapes gin-shop in Old Street Road, cost £100, and workmanship was by one of the first carvers in London. Three gin-shops have lately been fitted up in Lamb's Conduit Street at an expense, for the bar alone, of upwards of £2,000 each.'

Dickens of course has something to say, and gives the following description in *Sketches by Boz* published in 1836. '. . . the gay building with the fantastic-ally ornamental parapet, the illuminated clock, the plate-glass windows

69

surrounded by stucco rosettes, and its profusion of gas lights in richly gilt burners, is perfectly dazzling when contrasted with the darkness and dirt we have just left. The interior is even gayer than the exterior. A bar of french-polished mahogany elegantly carved, extends the whole width of the place; and there are two side aisles of great casks, painted green and gold, enclosed within a light brass rail, and bearing such descriptions as "Old Tom 549", "Young Tom 360", "Samson 1421"—the figures, we presume, agreeing with gallons, you understand. Beyond the bar is a lofty and spacious saloon, full of the same enticing vessels, with a gallery running round it, equally well furnished.'

The first Gin Palace, it is almost certain, dated from about 1830, for, to support Cruikshank, we have a witness giving evidence before a select committee in the House of Commons in 1834 saying: 'A public house nearly opposite my residence . . . was taken for a gin palace. It was converted into the very opposite of what it had been, a low dirty public house with only one doorway, into a splendid edifice, the front ornamental with pilasters, supporting a handsome cornice and entablatures and balustrades, and the whole elevation remarkably striking and handsome.'

A cutting from an unidentified newspaper about the same time, having commented on the handsomeness and *hauteur* of the race of barmaids, goes on to say: 'Thousands of pounds are spent on ornamenting these gin-shops, and gilded columns, and mahogany fronts, with silver bar engines are not uncommon. Quick returns, and increasing wealth are the lot of the proprietor. The House of which the above print (13, page 29) is a correct representation, is situated very near Holborn Hill and is first rate of its class.'

Yet another cutting, quoting from *England and America* 1833, is even more precise: 'At the shop of Messrs. Thompson and Fearon on Holborn Hill, gin is served by young women dressed up like the "*belle Limonadière*" of a Paris Coffee House and the establishment in all its parts is nearly as fine as Verey's or the Café de Paris. Every week, almost every day produces a new one, fitted up with spring doors, plate glass, carved mahogany or rosewood and polished brass.'

In 1890 there is more material from a discussion in the correspondence columns of an unidentified London newspaper on the subject. One correspondent states that 'the first Gin Palace was believed to be Fearon and Son at 94 Holborn Hill, nearly opposite St. Andrews Church which I remember as such sixty years ago.' Another goes further and says, 'Stephen Geary, architect and engineer who died . . . on August 28th 1854 aged seventy-five is said to have designed the first so-called Gin Palace in London. It seems probable that it was not earlier than 1830, as it is believed that the modern style of public houses, with larger windows and superior internal fittings, was not known before that period.'

Yet another source, H. Vizetelly in his *Glances back through Seventy Years*, published in 1893, says: 'It was near Field Lane that the first London Gin Palace was built. The polished mahogany counters, the garish bar fittings, the smartly painted vats, inscribed "Old Tom" and "Cream of the Valley", the rows of showy bottles of noyau and other cordials, and above all the immense blaze of gas light within and without these buildings as soon as dusk set in, were all so many novelties and came as a vision of splendour to the besotted denizens of the neighbouring slums. I remember that one of these so-called palaces had a second and lower counter for the accommodation of the children and juvenile thieves whom it counted among its patrons.'

Leaving this discussion on one side, however, it is clear that the Gin Palace sprang from an era of feverish development, the era of iron and steam, invention and exploitation of processes, free trade and free markets, cut-throat competition and untold riches for the survivors. Traditions were at a discount, anything new was good. Their development was due to the efforts of individual publicans and licensees, each trying to outdo his rival with all the tricks of showmanship and all the energy and zest of those hectic times. The Act of 1830 allowed anyone to open a beershop free of control by the Justices, and resulted in 45,000 of them appearing within eight years. The retailers of spirits met this competition with the Gin Palace.

But everyone could not grow rich. Millions of them found themselves engulfed in the sordid and squalid urban growths of established towns or expanding industrial areas. Transport did not exist for them and they lived in the shadow of mill, warehouse or counting house. The public house, gin shop, beerhouse was their ephemeral refuge from squalor, dirt, and failure.

The Gin Palace, solid yet ethereal, embodied in its brilliant lights and its lush decoration, wrought in the fine tradition of craftsmanship, all the glamour, finery and wealth that had escaped them, or, if they were climbing, was still out of reach.

For the publican-owner it was a gold-mine, for however glamorous or ethereal in the imagination of the customer, drink was a solid business proposition for him and every stone and pane of glass of his Gin Palace frontage might have been charged to advertising, if he had worried about income tax in those days.

E

71

The Victorian Pub. In passing from the Gin Palace that Cruikshank and his contemporaries describe to the Victorian pub, it is apparent that somehow there is either a gap in continuity or else there was a definite break. Perhaps the Victorian pub is an offspring of the 1851 Exhibition or perhaps it was a sign of increasing social stability, wealth and respectability. It may be that as our glimpses of its predecessors come to us mainly through the social reformer's eyes, the descriptions are overdrawn. It is even possible that our own eyes have so accustomed themselves to the triumphs of modern showmanship and display that we just do not see what our grandfathers saw with their palates undulled by a century's developments in mass selling techniques.

The most obvious change is the development of the horseshoe or 'O' shaped bar-counter, with its radiating partitions. The reasons for it were twofold. The first, common of course to the long bar of the Gin Palace, was the concentration of customers and the need to serve them as quickly as possible and as much as possible in the shortest space of time. This resulted in and encouraged the urban habit of perpendicular drinking. The second was the increasing respectability of Victorian society from top to bottom and, with it, a growing middle class which subdivided itself continually into multiple social strata. As we do not know who first hit on the answer, we can only surmise that some architect, or an astute publican, thought out this way of meeting the prejudices of his class-conscious customers. It was a solution to a traffic problem just as much as Haussmann's *Place de l'Etoile* or a Woolworth store today are practical solutions. The fact of this is easily lost in the whirl of decoration and self-advertisement which is the superficial, though important, side of a well thought out business proposition.

Here we have a remarkable piece of planning, perhaps not so much a break with tradition as an assimilation of tradition blossomed into a new species. Gone are the kitchen, the parlour and the piecemeal arrangement of the pre-nineteenth-century pub. Gone is the one long bar of the early Gin Palace. In their place is a plan for a pub *ab initio* designed within the bar-counter to provide easy circulations for the staff, easy access to the drinks and simple supervision for the landlord; outside it is a drinking space that could be subdivided by means of partitions radiating from the bar-counter into sections suited in size to the needs of the various social classes of customer.

Inside as well as outside, the Victorian pub often combined the dual qualities of decoration and utility. The mirrors, for instance, elaborately, and many of them beautifully, embossed and cut or painted with all manner of

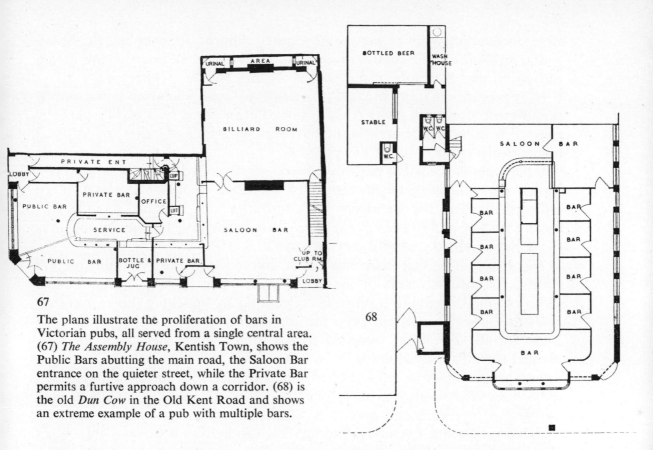

67

The plans illustrate the proliferation of bars in
Victorian pubs, all served from a single central area.
(67) *The Assembly House*, Kentish Town, shows the
Public Bars abutting the main road, the Saloon Bar
entrance on the quieter street, while the Private Bar
permits a furtive approach down a corridor. (68) is
the old *Dun Cow* in the Old Kent Road and shows
an extreme example of a pub with multiple bars.

gay subjects, had their practical aspect, for the publican could, with their
help, keep an eye on the many dark corners and alcoves or could see the faces
of customers whose backs were turned to him. In fact, when supervision of
pubs by the authorities became more stringent, they welcomed the fitting of
mirrors to walls for this very purpose. Mirrors also provided company for
the solitary customer and expanded the room when it might have felt
crowded.

The Victorian pub was a conscious effort to meet the changing drinking
habits of a growing middle class living in crowded urban communities. Their
social background was different from that of their fathers and grandfathers.
How the publicans and their architects tackled this problem is now considered
in greater detail.

But before passing to a more detailed inspection, a brief mention must be
made of its rather 'tonier' relation, the 'Grander than Home' pub. Its owner
would probably be hurt if we called his house a pub. Usually found in what

73

were once country towns and are now outer suburbs, it never had the heavy traffic problems of the central urban pub. Partly hotel and partly club with a restaurant and ballroom, its ambitions were definitely architectural.

In appearance it approximated to a wealthy, lavish Victorian home, which the urban rococo pub never tried to do, catering for a respectable, perhaps genteel, body of customers who preferred its 'upper class' marble and potted palms to the country pub atmosphere.

It had rooms instead of partitioned sections, flowered wallpapers, pictures, stained glass and leaded lights instead of decorated mirrors, and marble often replaced much of the mahogany. Its decoration was intended to reflect its social standing and to keep one on one's best behaviour. Its big city cousin is the 'Palatial' Hotel and with that we leave it.

The Room. The Victorian pub was a landmark in the evolution of pub design, for, in contrast with the earlier practice of linking, as required, a series of small rooms to a central service area by knocking down partition walls and opening up doorways, the customers' space and the service area were, for the first time, regarded as one unit, which then could be sub-divided to suit the local needs.

This great room was proportioned in accordance with current thought and techniques. The result was far loftier than pubs of an earlier date, achieving an effect of opulence and grandeur, which was increased by the vistas and impression of scale. Even from the smallest subdivision it was possible to get alluring glimpses of the rest of the room. This was achieved by stopping the partitions a few feet short of the ceiling, and not allowing the bar screens to obstruct entirely an oblique view along the length of the bar-counter. A ceiling, decorated in high relief and common to the whole room, provided a unifying feature which was all the more effective by being patterned rather than plain. The obscured glass partitions, although providing privacy and preventing a complete view, still transmitted light and atmosphere from adjoining bars and produced an effect of intrigue and mystery.

The bigger bars were often of sufficient size to be independent of the other parts of the room for this effect of scale, but the smaller bars would have indeed been box-like had they not had the dramatic focal point of the bar-counter and the ornamental bar-back or the island bar wagon. These formed a fourth wall which, though a barrier in the physical sense, was no barrier to the imagination.

It has not been possible to discover decoration specifications of the early examples of Victorian pubs, but it seems fairly certain that colours were mainly sombre but in warm tones, and the rich red brown of glossy french-polished mahogany, used for all wood surfaces, was probably the dominant colour. There were no curtains in the windows—no publican wanted to obscure from the passer-by the alluring glitter of his establishment—and no carpets on the floor. This, in fact, was usually plain boards in the public bar and frequently a mosaic pattern in the better parts of the house. Colour there was in these mosaics but insufficient to introduce a dominant theme. Colour there was, too, in a myriad of small objects, bottles, advertisements, copper measures, painted porcelain spirit containers. But these all added up to a kaleidoscopic scene of broken patterns which created its own effect, reflected a hundred times in the mirrors, themselves lavishly patterned to prevent an accurate reflection.

For the bar-counter and the monumental fitments behind the bar were reserved the full activities of the Victorian craftsmen of wood carving. Always in mahogany, the bar fitment rose from shelf to shelf, each supported by numerous columns and pilasters, to a classical crescendo at its summit, where cornices, minarets and architraves competed for pride of place, backed by panels of plain, embossed or brilliant cut mirror reflecting the glasses, bottles, containers, ferns and polished copper measures and funnels which crowded the shelves, to combine the functions of advertisement, display, decoration and merchandise rack.

The shape of these counters varied with the site and size of the room. If the site had, for example, a longer frontage than depth, the bar fitment would line the long back wall and the bar would be in shape a half lozenge somewhat flattened. In this case it approximated nearest to the earlier development of a bar—where it was a counter across a room. More usually in plan it would vary in shape between a horseshoe and a magnet, with the main fitment across the open end tacking on to the service and publican's quarters.

The longer this 'U' shape extended, the farther the server found himself from the stock. This resulted in the island fitment or wagon, which was a double-sided stock rack extending down the centre of the loop formed by the bar-counter thus reducing the distance that the staff had to walk to reach the stock.

These were not usually as elaborate as the main fitment but they were likewise loaded with a multiplicity of bottles, wine and spirit containers and glasses, with rows of spirit kegs, porcelain barrels and the like, each with its polished pipeline to service level.

In some cases, more usually in small pubs, this bar shape became an

75

unbroken elongated 'O' shape, the publican having no space for private quarters abutting on to the service area. In this event the wall fitment disappeared and the 'island' took its place.

The bar-counter, too, was often a most elaborate affair. Its only unrelieved surface was the top, made from huge slabs of solid mahogany, and polished repeatedly to retain its glossy richness, broken here and there by a group of beer-pulls (in decorated or plain porcelain or ebony and brass for all the world like soldier dolls on parade), fussy and fantastic glass spirit containers, polished mullers and shining brass lamp standards.

The real features of the bar-counter, at least in the saloon and private bars, were the 'snob screens' set in their framework of mahogany. These screens were embossed or brilliant-cut glass panels often gilded or painted with designs of birds and flowers, sometimes plain bevelled. They were small half-opened windows, pivoted on their vertical axes, and screened the frequenters of the saloon bar from the commoners drinking in the public bar. These were one of the characteristics of the Victorian bar and one of the most decorative. When they first came into use is not clear, though they probably date from about 1860.

The framework holding these screens was sometimes a light flimsy structure of turned and fluted columns, but more often was a monumental affair of massive mahogany pilasters and scrolls, curving out into the room with the bar-counter, and supporting a shelf for glasses with a little fence of polished wrought or fretted brasswork round it to stop the glasses falling off. The public bar, too, often had such a fitment, as the shelf was a handy position for drinking vessels, but it was a plainer fitment with no swivelling screens.

All this equipment undoubtedly required a great deal of maintenance, but this was not a problem in those days. To keep the woodwork, brasswork, glass and mirrors always spick, span and glistening was the pride and joy of the publican and his staff.

The Saloon Bar. Approached from a side alley, from the less frequented street of a corner site or by a screened corridor within the pub itself, the entrance to the saloon bar was usually withdrawn from the full glare of the frontal gaslight. Its frequenters, the artisans, the white collar brigade and others who had social positions to maintain, could thus slip in almost unobserved to join their fellow socialites or mingle with the racier group of regulars who had no reputation to lose. There they could pass the time beyond the reach of their wives and out of sight perhaps of cronies of other days who used the public bar.

The saloon bar was the decorative and financial highlight of the Victorian pub. A great deal of money was spent on building pubs, but in the saloon bar money was literally no object, no expense was spared, the solid achievements of Victorian craftsmen were positively poured out in fashioning a scene of lavish opulence.

As the entrance door with its protective frosted panel embossed with the legend 'Saloon Bar' shut behind one, the first impression was of a wall of mirror glass, semi-obscured by an intricate embossed and cut pattern, divided into panels, each framed in mahogany, reflecting in an infinitely broken and confused pattern the lights and features of the room. Sometimes these larger panels covered the wall to a height of twelve feet or so and then, usually, the lower part of them only would be decorated, leaving the upper part unobscured. Sometimes their smooth contours would be interrupted by a little mosaic surround of mirror and mahogany. When these mirrors were carried round a curved corner a very interesting effect was achieved.

Breaking into this wall there was usually a large open fireplace, surmounted by a towering and highly elaborate mahogany overmantel rising to the ceiling and enthroning the inevitable clock, which might, perhaps, be set in mahogany intricacies or clutched by a bevy of whirling metal maidens.

Equally elaborate and dramatic, the bar-counter opposite would curve out into the room carrying its secluding array of little screens, mahogany supports, and top shelf garnished with polished brass, bearing its load of glasses, ferns and flowerpots. Beyond there would probably be a glimpse of the length of the bar, a glimpse into space, flanked by the magnificent bar fitment.

Shutting off the view from the private bar adjoining was a partition, panelled in mahogany to a height of four or five feet and, above, a mahogany framework surrounding panels of embossed and brilliant-cut glass, sometimes rectangular, sometimes curved shapes, and frequently to be seen in panels that resembled the plan view of a Victorian pub with its partitions radiating from it.

Beneath the wall mirrors and partition glass there were built-in seats well padded in horsehair, upholstered in black leather and dimpled all over with those retaining buttons reminiscent of ancient first-class railway compartments. Groups of similarly upholstered, upright mahogany chairs clustered round heavy cast-iron circular tables with little brass rails encircling their polished mahogany or marble tops. They were heavy, solid tables, with bulging legs bearing all manner of effigies on their curving knees, fully proof against

69

70   a   b   c   d

The Victorian pub was a business proposition. The service plan was as important
as the decoration. (69) Part of the service space in *The Assembly House*, Kentish
Town. (70) **a, b, c,** and **d** illustrate the basic bar-counter shapes evolved for the Victorian
pub, the choice depending on the site. In the centre is the 'island' or 'wagon.'

78

71

72

73

74

(71–74) George Cruikshank, almost alone among contemporary illustrators, has left impressions of the early Gin Palaces that flourished among the urban slums of London's 1830's. Since he was preaching against the horrors of gin-drinking he undoubtedly caricatured them, but he nevertheless shows that the use of casks, containers and similar equipment was an essential part of their decoration. From a cautionary series entitled 'The Gin Shop', published in 1855.

75

77

The Victorian Gin Palace was planned as one large room, subdivided by partitions but unified by the relief pattern of the ceilings as in (75), *The Crown and Sceptre*, Great Titchfield Street. The ornate mahogany 'wagon' screens the Saloon Bar public from the rest, though usually 'snob screens' were mounted on the counter for this purpose, as in *The Eagle*, Camden Town (76), and the *Bunch of Grapes*, Brompton Road (77). Those in *The Prince Alfred*, Maida Vale (78), have a particularly magnificent mahogany framework.

76

(79) In the Victorian Saloon Bar decorated glass was used to soften the glare, heighten the theatrical effect and enclose the room with walls which were, in effect, no barriers at all. The glowing patterns of curling, twisting tracery seem suspended in space like man-made cobwebs caught in the beam of a lantern. The polished surface of the bar-counter, devoid

of the usual mahogany superstructure curves, gracefully out from the bar-back, a solid
down-to-earth contrast to the Christmas decorations above. The Saloon Bar in *The Red Lion*,
Duke of York Street, St. James's, is a perfect example, except for bomb-damage, of the
small Victorian Gin Palace at its best.

(80) The theme of mahogany and glass, the one curving and twisting in a complex of free but semi-classic forms to frame the glowing glittering pattern of the other, is repeated throughout the Victorian Gin Palace: a bar window at *The Morpeth Arms*, Millbank.

81 *(left)*

82 *(right)*

83 *(left)*

84 *(right)*

(81) Part of the Saloon Bar, and (82), a Private Bar in *The Assembly House*, Kentish Town, show the intricately carved mahogany screen framing the partitions. (83) *The Red Lion*, St. James's is on a smaller scale. (84) a mahogany and brass counter stand in *The Black Horse*, Rathbone Place.

85

86

87

Two examples of the 'island' fitments so typical of the Victorian pub plan. (85) *The Unicorn*, Shoreditch, is a good example of the long centre fitment enclosed by an elongated 'O' shaped bar-counter. (86) *The Boston*, Kentish Town, has an unusual triangular structure enclosing an office. (87) is a view down the corridor in *The Red Lion*, St. James's, so characteristic of the approach to the Saloon Bar.

the lurch of any customer who might be less steady on his pins than they.

Dotted about, oblivious of the lay-out of the 'room', sheathed in Lincrusta and crowned with corinthian capitals, cast-iron supports supplied a practical note to the profusion and served as useful props for the perpendicular drinker.

The plan of the saloon bar was not always regular, for the snug and the alcove were much appreciated by the regular groups who preferred to sit and keep themselves to themselves. These broken lines multiplied still further the broken pattern of the decoration and added to the cosiness of the atmosphere.

The Public Bar. In the Victorian pub, the public bar, from the decorative point of view, comes rather a poor last to all the other bars. The customer paid less, had no desire to be screened from anyone, not even from his wife who came with him, and did not mind anyone knowing it. He could come in his working clothes and jostle his fellows without causing offence or undue notice, which meant far more in the nineteenth century than it does today. Towns were not the clean places that they are now, and the labourer did all the heavy and dirty jobs in his everyday clothes, unprotected by overalls and special clothing or by hygienic packaging.

For these reasons alone it would have been unpractical to furnish the public bar with padded seats and the other refinements of the saloon bar. Mirrors were hardly appropriate, for not only did they run considerable danger on the rowdy nights, but a man prefers to look at himself when he is dressed for the shock. Lastly, of course, the publican spent as little as he could on this section, because he knew that if the liquor was all right and he and his staff played their part, he would get his customers just the same.

Glamour there was in the finery of the bar-back, which the public bar shared with the others, in the semi-obstructed views of other parts of the house and in glimpses of other customers in other bars. The peregrinations of the barmaids or the appearance of the publican himself from behind a plush curtain, and the buzz of voices from beyond the partitions, all linked the public bar to this other world.

The decoration, apart from those features already described, was limited almost entirely to embossed glass panels in the door, mahogany partitions with an architrave and a few whirligigs on the top, possibly a few frosted brilliant-cut panels beneath it, but quite often with none, a mahogany framed bench with a curving perforated bent-wood seat like an old-time tram seat along one wall, and perhaps one small heavy table.

The public bar was always nearest to the traffic outside. For instance, on a corner site it would usually have an entrance at the corner and a window flanking each street. It therefore boasted at least two heavy brass rails, with the customary triple gas brackets blazing their warm invitation to passers-by above the simple embossing of the plate-glass windows. The mahogany bar-counter, which it shared with the other bars, must have looked stark and naked to a visitor from the saloon, and the floor devoid of mosaic would offer only spittoons like little islands in a sea of sawdust, and they were hardly decorative. However, this bareness was as it should be, when one remembers that the grandsire of the public bar was the alehouse kitchen.

Decorated Glass. The most remarkable decorative feature of the Victorian pub was undoubtedly the embossed and brilliant-cut glass and mirrors, used for wall decoration, partitions, bar-backs and bar screens.

This form of glass decoration was a product of the nineteenth century and rapidly became an important addition to an old and noble craft. Now, as with all crafts, those skilled in it are fast disappearing, with few trained to take their places.

The raw material was plate-glass. In the '40's an excise duty imposed on it many years before was withdrawn, and this, combined with Paxton's use of it in the Crystal Palace at the 1851 Exhibition, focused attention on its possibilities.

Decoration, whatever the process, consisted in obscuring sections of clear glass but retaining its translucence. Ground glass, the earliest form of obscured glass, was made by the laborious process of rubbing fine emery powder over the clear plate with a large glass muller. If a design or lettering was required, the surface of the glass was coated with brunswick black, the design was traced on through the black and fluoric acid was poured over it. The brunswick black acted as a resist and protected the part to be left unaffected, and the acid etched the design where the glass was exposed.

This method was used as early as the 1830's, for Dickens refers to inscribed ground glass door panels in his description of Gin Palaces of that date.

The next development was the application of brilliant-cutting to large sheets of plate-glass. Brilliant, or deep, cutting of glass is, of course, an old technique, and had been used for years in decorating glassware. It was possible to cut small panes of glass in the same way, but large panels were far too heavy to control over the long periods required to work them. It was not until 1850 that Mark Bowden, of Bristol, developed an apparatus, introduced from the United States, with an overhead arrangement of counterbalances from which the heavy glass plate was suspended, thus enabling the operator to handle it with ease. He then pressed the glass against a rotating stone wheel and manipulated it to cut the pattern required. The cut was subsequently smoothed and polished.

It was an extremely intricate process calling for considerable skill, as the wheels required for different effects varied in diameter and in section, and themselves required frequent grinding to restore the cutting edge. The patterns possible by this process were confined to straight or gently curving lines and dots, though naturally the depth could be varied.

Brilliant-cutting was also used for lettering, and it is an interesting fact that the easiest type of lettering to cut was the so-called fishtail half-Gothic, so typical of some of the brewers' mirror glass advertisement panels of that time. Plain block letters were the most difficult, and, for that reason, not popular. This process probably achieves its most beautiful effects in conjunction with mirror glass, for the gently curving deep-cut scroll patterns stand out silvered against the clear reflections. Gilding on the cut or embossed pattern is also seen occasionally.

The earlier designs used in embossing were frequently renderings of acanthus foliage, vine leaves, hops and sheaves of barley, though later complicated scroll designs became popular. Birds, too, were a favourite subject particularly for the small panels of the bar 'snob screens'. Back painting of glass, and particularly of mirrors, with all manner of lush scenes from storks and water-lilies to highly decorated house signs in bright enamel colours, was introduced about the '70's for wall decoration and, of course, the brewers' advertising mirrors in this technique are quite common.

All the embossed glass during the nineteenth century was done with these three processes, employed either singly or in conjunction with one another, for no technical change appeared till 1900, when 'white acid', a mixture of fluoric acid and soda, replaced the tedious grinding process. As before pure acid was used to etch designs, but more variation was now possible by varying the degree of obscurity and, therefore, the relative tones achieved with each operation. Triple or French-embossing, developed shortly afterwards, permitted a third tone to be added. This last process also employed fluoric and white acid and to that extent was not new. It was the art of applying the acids that opened up new possibilities, for, by making several exposures to acid, by varying its strength and the period of exposure to it, it was possible to emboss designs in tones known technically as 'white', 'half-tone' and 'bright'. Between each exposure to acid, the part of the design not to be treated had, of course, to be protected with the resist.

Two factors sounded the death knell of embossing. The first was the changing fashion which brought leaded lights into popularity and, of course, new wall treatments in other materials also had their effect. The second was the technique of sand-blasting.

Sand-blasting, which ultimately cheapened the cost of obscuring plate-glass where quantity production was needed, was first patented in 1870, but took time to gain ground because, for some time, it was impossible to produce a design, there being no suitable resist. The process itself was revolutionary, as it operated in the same way as a spray gun, fine sand being blown under pressure against the glass plate. Ultimately zinc stencils were used to cover those parts of the plate to be left clear and decoration became possible, varying densities being obtained by using different grades of sand.

Now the race of men who brought glass embossing to a highly skilled craft has almost disappeared; their skill is going with them, but they will have a worthy monument in the Victorian pub.

Graining and Marbling. The decorative crafts of graining and marbling are neither peculiar to England nor English pubs. Yet it is almost impossible to find a pub without examples of graining either inside or out. Marbling, much used in the early Victorian Gin Palaces, is not nearly so common today.

The use of both crafts can be traced back to the Greeks and Egyptians if necessary, but, as we are interested in their application to pubs, it appears that we do not have to go further back than about 1800 in the case of graining, while marbling was probably introduced into Gin Palaces about 1830.

Both processes were, of course, developed originally as a means of imitating more cheaply the genuine article, but grainers and marblers and their supporters have maintained for long that the craft required such technical skill, and was brought to such perfection, that it is now no longer a matter of mere imitation, despite the castigations of Ruskin. There are very sound reasons for both processes, as a broken surface pattern can stand up to hard wear better than a plain flat paint, and can, moreover, be touched up again less obviously, both important matters in a pub.

In 1827 one Nathaniel Whittock wrote a book on graining, and he says that for the previous ten years graining had taken quite a hold and there were few inns even then which did not have graining to show on doors, shutters and wainscots. From that date the craft improved steadily in technique till, in the mid-century, its two greatest exponents, Thomas Kershaw of Bolton, and John Taylor of Birmingham, brought it to its highest peak of craftsmanship, establishing a tradition carried on by others such as W. G. Sutherland of Manchester, Claque of Preston, Cloak of

London, and McPherson, who travelled all over the country as a free-lance.

English oak has always been the favourite wood among English grainers, partly from tradition and partly due to its great variety of colour and markings, establishing, in fact, a kitchen vernacular. The more fancy woods were not considered suitable for pubs and so, apart from some examples of mahogany and teak, oak graining, particularly in the 'Home from Home' type, is by far the most popular. The choice was usually narrowed from the range of oaks available, i.e., heartwood, quartered, fumed, pollard and root, to the first two. The resulting patterns varied in colour and treatment with the craftsman's skill, but there are few customers these days who cast a critical eye on the grainer's workmanship, if they notice it at all. To the 'casual' or 'regular' layman it is probably enough that it serves its purpose in helping to create a pleasant pub.

The traditional tools of the grainer and marbler are numerous, and their names, odd-sounding to the ears of the uninitiated, have been in use for generations. Sash tool, jamb duster, flogger, badger softener, over-grainer, pencil over-grainer, improvised grainer, veining horn, check roller, flat fitch, fan fitch, all have their place in the craftsman's bag.

The technique of graining and marbling can only be hinted at. It is a subject for the technical expert, and, like all crafts, each expert has his own methods for achieving the results he requires. It is sufficient to say that a ground colour is applied first, approximating to the lightest shade in the wood or marble, and this is followed by a water, an oil, or in earlier days a spirit stain, as a medium into which the colours are gradually worked. The figuring is then done with combs and the other special gadgets at the grainer's disposal, not forgetting that most valuable of craftsman's tools, the human thumb. It is also interesting to note that one of the traditional ingredients, in particular for oak graining, is that excellent commodity, good English ale.

The tradition of graining is today one of the last remnants of the country pub vernacular that is still practised in urban pubs, even pubs in the Gin Palace tradition. Old pubs which could have been ruined in the name of modernity, as were earlier ones, by the craze for glazed tiles, are still being treated this way both outside and inside, at least in the public bar.

From graining, colours have derived, which are now used by themselves without any attempt at a broken surface. Thus there are light, medium and dark oak colours, teak colour, mahogany colour and chocolate colours undoubtedly related to mahogany. These appear usually inside the pub as

91

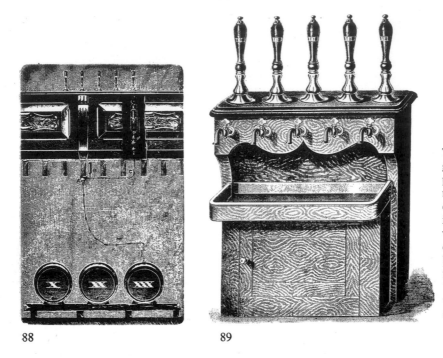

The technique of graining, though not peculiar to the pub, might well have died out long ago but for its traditional use in the vernacular pub decoration. (89) is a beer engine from a bar-fitter's catalogue of 1890. Its essential working details are shown in (88).

88   89

dadoes and friezes, or on the bar-front and on furniture. Sometimes they appear in the oddest places, as in the case of one brewery which uses a mahogany colour as a background for the gilt-lettered sign which they have standardized on the outside of many of their pubs.

This tradition of graining and wood colours should be studied by the pub designer, not with the intention of copying from the past, though there are many new pubs that would be improved thereby, but as an indication of the colours that are satisfactory and traditional in a pub. Graining also shows how a flat surface can be broken and made interesting, in the same way that le Corbusier has used enlarged photographs of microcosms for wall decoration.

Walls and Ceilings. Embossed wallpapers of one kind and another are to be seen in almost all the Victorian pubs which still exist today. Ceilings, friezes, dadoes, cornices, even supporting columns, have their jacket of embossed Lincrusta, Anaglypta, Tynecastle or Cameoid, in high or low relief, sometimes painted over or varnished, and sometimes just mellowed to an orangey coffee colour by nicotine fumes.

Some of the high relief ceilings are excellent in design and, as mentioned earlier, provide a unifying effect to the room by carrying the scale outside the confines of each separate bar. Low relief in ceilings often fails in this function and fits in better on the smaller surfaces of dadoes and friezes.

It is not always easy to the untrained eye to decide which patent embossing process has been used; in fact it is difficult to tell the high relief work from plaster in some cases for which, of course, it is a substitute.

Embossed materials of this kind developed relatively late in the nineteenth century and the various names by which they are known indicate the different processes by which they were made, their composition, and the decorative effect achieved by them. It is unlikely that wallpapers of any kind were used in pubs before 1841, the date when roller printing of paper on a calico printing machine was first introduced on a commercial scale by the Potters of Darwen. Before this time, wallpapers were hand-blocked and expensive, and certainly beyond the means of any publican unless he owned a Gin Palace.

Tynecastle was the first embossed wall-covering in the field, developed in the early seventies by William Scott Morton. Leather was used first, and then a few years later, canvas, which gave it a slightly rough 'old' surface texture. This was followed by Tynecastle vellum for friezes and mouldings, both types being in solid relief. Lincrusta or Lincrusta-Walton, as it was known after its inventor, was introduced in 1877, and, likewise in solid relief, was made mainly of solidified linseed oil on a canvas backing. Ten years later the canvas backing was replaced by paper which provided a more flexible and resilient material, having the great advantage of being waterproof. It was used mainly to imitate wood carving and leather.

Cameoid, a third process invented in 1888 by an employee of Walton's, was not developed for another ten years lest it compete with Lincrusta, but from then on it achieved considerable success, as it could be pressed out of paper, was hollow-backed, unlike the previous processes, and was a cheaper material. Its eventual exploitation was probably due to the success achieved by a new rival, Anaglypta, the biggest threat to Walton's Lincrusta; it was made by embossing paper pulp in the wet stage. It was hollow-backed, but since the fibres were not strained by the pressing, it had no tendency to alter in shape once set. Patterns in very high relief were possible and for ceilings it soon superseded Lincrusta because it was light in weight, moderate in cost, and being made in small squares was comparatively easy to handle. Its inventor, T. J. Palmer, who also worked for Walton at one time, took out his first patents in 1887 and employed, among others, C. F. A. Voysey and Gilbert Bayes to design for him. A later improvement of the process, using hydraulic presses and malleable pulp, enabled even higher relief to be achieved.

93

Much of such work still to be found has been painted or varnished many times since it was put up, and none can be seen in anything approaching its first freshness. It is, however, very hard wearing, and the original wall-covering continues, although the white and cream tones wilt under the action of nicotine, and the dark greens, browns and mahogany reds of the dadoes and friezes lose their richness.

THE TRADITION SUMMED UP

The foregoing account of how the main types of traditional pub, 'the Home from Home' or rural, and the theatrical urban type developed, brings the process approximately to the end of the nineteenth century. This point marks the end of an era, determined not so much by the nice round date as by the fact that it was in the '90's that the big breweries started in real earnest to buy up the pubs.

The evolutionary process by which it is suggested these visual elements in the pub took shape is logical enough in the light of the evidence available. But since not one of the millions of their customers has ever, as far as can be discovered, endeavoured to set down for posterity any account such as this, the conclusions drawn at this late date must inevitably be based on circumstantial evidence. In any case, dates are of little use except where they indicate the appearance of a new technique—Lincrusta for instance—and enable one to say that before such and such a date Lincrusta could not have been used in pubs, because it just did not exist.

Again, the process by which the alehouse kitchen became a country pub, or a country pub became an urban pub depended not so much on the time element as on the period in which that particular part of the countryside came under the influence of urban ideas or actually became a part of a built-up area.

From a purely historical point of view, more facts would certainly have been valuable, but even without them the picture is nevertheless fairly clear. Beginning as a wayside cottage or farmhouse where passers-by were allowed to refresh themselves in the kitchen—the family living room-cum-working room of those days—the process of specialization crept in, and the emphasis gradually changed from that of a spare-time business into a whole-time one. The kitchen for a time remained a kitchen with its fireplace and overmantel

(90) An urban vernacular for the Public Bar has evolved from the Victorian plan and traditional decoration: *The Gloucester Arms*, Marylebone.

94

E*

94

97

93

96

95

(91, 92) The Public Bar in an urban pub, still with its wood colours and simple built-in bench. Half a century's influence by the Victorian Gin Palace has been slight: *The Gloucester Arms*, Marylebone. (93) *The Cricketers' Arms*, Bill Quay, Newcastle, emphasizes the same elements. *The Crown and Anchor*, New Cross (94) has an unusual combination of the kitchen vernacular and its product, the urban vernacular in adjoining rooms. (95), the Public Bar in *The Assembly House*, Kentish Town, has simple fittings in contrast to the glitter of the Saloon Bar glimpsed beyond. (96), *The Red Lion*, St. James's, and (97), *The Crown and Anchor*, New Cross, both illustrate a shape that originated in the high-backed settle and is here adapted for partition ends.

(98) The influence of the Victorian Saloon Bar gradually had its effect on the Public Bar: *The Yorkshire Stingo*, Marylebone, shows this Gin Palace backwash. Engraved glass is still a unique feature of the Victorian Gin Palace. It was not unusual for the sign of the pub to be introduced into the design of the interior in this material: (99) is from *The Ship*, Greenwich, and was one of the finest examples of its kind. *The Ship* was destroyed in an air raid.

100

101

Engraved glass designs generally had floral or bird themes reproduced by the acid or by the brilliant-cut techniques on plain or silver-backed plate glass. Often the two processes were combined as in the mirrors in (100) *The Assembly House*, Kentish Town. (101) is another example of a house sign—acid embossed—at *The Eagle*, Camden Town. (102), a glass and mahogany partition in *The White Swan*, Pimlico, suggests that the basic Victorian bar-counter plan has somehow crept into the decoration.

102

101

(103) The dark outline to the engraved mirror in *The Boston*, Kentish Town, shows clearly the bold sweeps and the terminal dots and fishtails associated with the brilliant-cut process. (104), in *The St. Stephen's Tavern*, Westminster, shows the far more versatile acid technique at its best.

(105) This unusually simple detail from *The Red Lion*, St. James's, shows the soft and luminous quality possible with acid-embossing on mirror glass.

(106) The ceiling of the Victorian Gin Palace was traditionally in a relief pattern and usually, the bigger the pub, the bolder the design. Anaglypta or Tynecastle were most commonly employed for effects such as this in *The Black Lion*, Kilburn. Few of the old gas lights still exist, the blaze of which used to announce the Gin Palace from far off. On the opposite page is one of the many patent fittings designed for the purpose (107).

115

116

The fittings and detail, still to be seen in the Victorian pub are manifold and fascinating. The elaborate brass rails with triple gas-burner (108), were always set in the windows to blaze a welcome to passers-by.
Decorated porcelain beer-pulls in heavy brass mounts (109) have not yet entirely vanished. (110) The ornate grille acts as a unique screen to the Ladies' Bar of *The Markham Arms*, Chelsea. (111) and (112) show details of the carved and turned supports on the bar-counter.
Furniture in the Victorian pub was on the whole functional rather than ornate. In the Public Bar, scrubbed tables, benches (113) and perforated bentwood seats (114) were standard. (115) Even in the Saloon Bar, seats were often little more than upholstered versions of the last. (116) Bar stools are more recent but this functional example is in the true pub tradition.

117

118

119

120

Lettering, and especially the forms adopted for the brewers' advertisement mirrors, became one of the most effective forms of pub decoration. The type of letter illustrated by the word 'stout' in (117) and (119) is a form that came easily to the process of brilliant-cutting; it was taken over and elaborated by the embosser, who added gilding and bright colours. (118) and (120) show sign-writing technique and applied lettering; in (118) the bold sans-serif capitals are painted on the glass, and are not related at all to the art of glass-making. (120) again is a different style, found almost exclusively on the outsides of windows, the solid letters being cemented onto the glass.

121

122

(121) A simple cast-iron
capital of the kind found in
almost every Victorian pub.
(122) A Saloon Bar clock
lodged at the apex of the
fantastically elaborate
mahogany carving of the
bar-back. The face is almost
an anti-climax.

123

124

Cast-iron furniture, though often elaborate, remained solid and practical like (123) the typical ram's-head table. (124) The carved house sign is in *The Bunch of Grapes*, Brompton Road.

hung with all the cooking and serving utensils, its solid furniture, and its bare plaster walls. Subsequent additions, such as the tap-room store, an inglenook with high-backed settles, denoting the gradual change-over from kitchen to pub were made in the same terms; so, when the kitchen as a cooking-room disappeared and left the kitchen in its new guise of drinking room—or perhaps tap-room, the barrels, bottles, jugs, measures and mugs took over the decorative function of the cooking utensils, but instead of appearing over the fireplace they were stood or hung in the servery. The servery was gradually opened up, ceased to be a little room on its own and became part of the main room with a counter across it. Any publican with an orderly mind ranged his containers and drinking vessels in an orderly manner, where he could go to them automatically. The illustrations show that by the early nineteenth century, an element of conscious embellishment had begun to appear. So the kitchen overmantel gave birth to the bar-back, and the use of essential kitchen equipment as decoration was inherited by the pub.

The same principle appears in the eighteenth-century urban gin shop—witness the rows of barrels; and again in the early Gin Palace—the Gin 'Temple' of Cruikshank's time. In these, far more containers were used than in the country pub, for they specialized in a far wider range of drinks, mainly spirits, and needed far greater quantities. The decorative idea became competitive and spread to bright colours and gilt, highly-polished rosewood and mahogany woodwork and brasswork. In the Victorian saloon bar this process continued, decorated glass was introduced, woodwork became ebullient in the bar structure and partitions, embossed ceilings and dadoes appeared and the containers which now included glasses and bottles became more varied and colourful. But it was not all display, for beneath this fantastic, exotic scene it is clear that considerable thought was given to planning. In it, the one long counter that characterized the early Gin Palace was abandoned and gave way to the horseshoe bar in varying forms. The drinking space was split up into small bars, alcoves and snugs, which borrowed direct from the kitchen's chimney-corner tradition, clearly because the club element of the country pub was reasserting itself in the towns, where people did not always want to stand in a milling mob, swilling their liquor till they fell down. So another aspect of the urban pub can be shown to originate in the kitchen tradition.

The Victorian saloon or Gin Palace—though in its own way a work of art and for that reason alone worthy of preservation—is nevertheless a period piece, something that we do not expect to see repeated, but it does possess an inner propriety even when it appears to be completely irrational and fantastic and it would be a tragedy if the idea that florid decoration is out of date or not in good taste should lead to the final liquidation of all Gin Palaces in favour of the so-called modern.

The much older pub tradition that lies behind it is to be found in every village and country town. It is a visual tradition based essentially on a very plain interior with modest embellishments; but it is plain in the sense that grained oak or teak are plain; it is plain in the sense that it is not striving after an effect, but is unconsciously a functional synthesis of natural colours and shapes that are living and not just arid and pointless. Its solid furniture and other woodwork have the colours of oak and teak and mahogany whether in their natural form, grained to simulate them or painted with the flat colours that derive from these woods; its walls are plaster white, stone and earth colours, reminiscent of the kitchen and farmhouse. Light and shade is supplied by the points of light that reflect from the dark, undulating rows of bottles, from the polished tankards and the mirrors; brilliance and flashes of bright colour are contributed by pieces of brasswork, bottle-labels, bright advertisements and lettering; form by the casks, by the china rum and whisky jars behind the counter, by the beer-pulls upon it, by the shining scrubbed tables and the stuffed fish in their glass cases.

From this tradition a vernacular evolved, which has been adopted almost universally for those urban pubs which did not cater for the saloon bar customer and even in the public bar of the Gin Palace this same essential simplicity prevailed, in spite of the ostentation a few yards away.

There has of course been much interchange of ideas between the country and the urban pubs, for the two types of pub did not evolve independently. The alehouse kitchen borrowed its modest bar from the urban pub and probably, unconsciously, some of its profusion as well. In fact, it was this borrowing from the urban tradition that turned what was essentially a farmhouse kitchen into a country pub, and then changed it—if indeed it changed again—into the small urban vernacular pub or public bar, so that this, even when slightly rococo'd by the Gin Palace backwash or touched by the landlord's whimsy, is the true functional vernacular. This is the pub tradition which stands behind brewer, publican, designer and customer or whoever has the task of merging new requirements with the traditional pattern.

THE TRADITION BROKEN

The pub tradition played little part in the many pubs built between the wars. Attempts to replace it with 'pseudo' and modern styles failed for various reasons described in this chapter.

The beginning of the twentieth century heralded the disappearance of the traditional element from many of the older pubs, and its virtual exclusion from the design of new ones. The reasons for this were many, and most of them, in the light of the times, practical.

The brewers, who had between them acquired some ninety per cent of the pubs by 1910, were only too conscious of the dingy reputation that clung to their properties and to the idea of 'drink' in general. This fact was brought home to them by a host of well-organized reformers who were all out to close them down, the police who frequently found their supervisory duties somewhat onerous and the magistrates who were always in a position to refuse to renew a licence if all was not well.

The course they chose was the only one open to them short of succumbing; they set about making the pubs respectable, and ushered in the 'improved public house'. The improvements, it is true, were mainly concerned with amenities, management and supervision, but in the process of shedding the nineteenth-century reputation, they also shed the nineteenth-century form.

At this point the architect enters the foreground of the scene. He has been present, of course, somewhere in the background, throughout the nineteenth century, but the total effect of the Victorian pub was not the personal contribution of the architect; it was a popular style, and, at the most, he himself was only responsible for some new variation of a continuing tradition. But that tradition came to an end when the pub became just another type of building, an architectural programme to which the architect, dependent on his own resources, had to apply his inventive powers. The practical restrictions that he was up against were certainly numerous and complex requiring him to conform to the laws of local authorities, planning authorities, police and finally to run the gauntlet of the licensing Justices at the Brewster Sessions. But it is evident that, in reaching his solution he was by no means hamstrung by them, as the accompanying illustrations show. The very names applied

Brewer's Tudor was a style seized on by certain
brewers and their architects in the 1920's, in order
to graft 'tradition' on to new pubs. The result
had no relation either to architectural honesty or to
the real pub tradition. (125) and (126), the Saloon Bar,
(127) and (128), the Public Bar, of *The Driftbridge
Hotel*, Ewell.

129

130

131

Brewer's Pseudish includes all other forms that ape past architectural styles. In general these favoured a rustic theme. There is the sophisticated dairy style of (129), a pleasant, light and airy room, but never a pub. There is the tithe-barn technique of (130), again a pleasant room, though hardly a sincere piece of contemporary architecture. And lastly the self-conscious ingle-nook of (131), with its fantastic barley-sugar supports, its pseudo beaten ironwork and accentuated brickwork. (129) The Saloon Bar, *The Drum*, Cockington, Devon. (130) The Saloon Bar, *The Woodman*, Blackfen, Kent. (131) *The Plough*, Sutton, Surrey.

132

133

134

117

Brewer's Modern. When the attempt was made to create a pub in the contemporary architectural idiom, the choice lay between a streamlined modernistic model, a form modernistic on the bar side and homely on the other, and various forms of 'Georgian'. All lacked any sign of the urban vernacular. The jazz effects of (132) are already dated; the gleaming black and chromium bar-counter of (133) is too machine-like for its well-mannered but wishy-washy surroundings. (134) is a conscientious piece of architecture, but it fails, as the others do. (132) *The Avenue Bar*, Shaftesbury Avenue. (133) *The Duke of Wellington*, Kenton. (134) *The Golden Lion*, Wolverhampton.

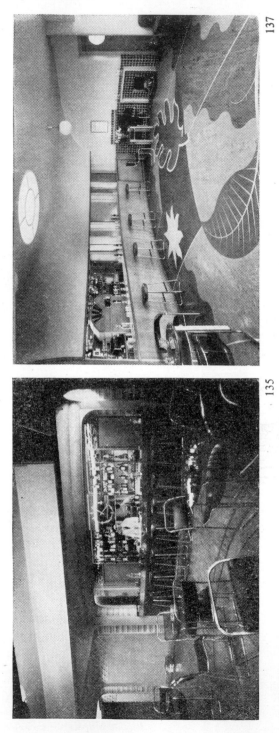

137

136

135

Road House. The city Cocktail Bar and the Road House owed something to the tradition of the Gin Palace and quite a lot to the transitory spirit of their age. They were often characterized by chromium and plastics, bright colours and display lighting, but missed the decorative possibilities of their own stock-in-trade. (136), the Cocktail Bar, is an example of this sterile approach. (135) suffers from the same trouble. (137), the Saloon Bar of *The Prospect Inn*, Minster, Kent, reflects the best of the contemporary idiom, but has still not solved the problem of designing a pub.

(138) The Public Bar in *The Norbury Hotel*, illustrates the 'Georgian' tendency so evident in pub interior design just prior to the war. It shows the large bleak interior that resulted from the attempt to design pubs that would not look like pubs. Sometimes indistinguishable from post offices or banks, they deny the whole pub tradition and only succeed in discouraging the customer from joining his cronies round the kitchen chimney corner.

139

140

Brewer's Georgian. The complete break with the pub's visual tradition, as exemplified particularly by the 'Georgian' interior, was not primarily a reaction against the tradition as such, but rather just one part of the process of making the pub respectable. (139) Saloon Bar in *The Bull*, East Sheen. (140) Public Bar in *The Rising Sun*, Fetcham. (141) Saloon Bar in *The Park Royal Hotel*.

141

to these solutions, Brewer's Tudor, Brewer's Pseudish, Brewer's Modern and Road House, two of them already in popular currency, indicate the uncertainty with which he has approached the problem, and his unwillingness to stand on his own two feet, squarely to face it. The Tudorbethan phase and the other period imitations that followed were not peculiar to pub architecture by any means but they were seized on by the pub architect at a time when architecture was very much in a state of uncertainty. It was in fact a tacit acceptance that an important element of tradition was bound up with the pub, and by jumping a matter of three centuries they resurrected the idea of the traditional English inn which at that time was being rediscovered and endowed with 'ye olde halo' to no mean purpose.

So the pubs went Tudor and embraced all the incongruities inevitable when sterilized medieval frills are draped round twentieth-century mass-production and amenities. It was a formula in which was wrapped a collection of theatrical shams, which bore no relation whatever either to architectural honesty or the true functional tradition of the pub. Moreover, the 'tradition' reproduced was merely a figment of the imagination and had no roots what-ever in the excellent one that existed. The same criticisms apply to the 'pseudisms' that followed when the Tudorbethan novelty began to wear off. In general, these harped on a rustic note, sometimes as a faithful piece of reconditioning of a tithe-barn, sometimes as a less faithful example of rustic feudalism and even a modernized peasant style. Whatever the phase, it did not last long for the simple reason that none of them had roots in the real tradition.

When the pseudo styles were cast to one side and the attempt was made to create a pub in the contemporary architectural idiom, several parallel paths were followed. The choice seems to have been either a modernistic model of about 1930 which long ago looked tawdry and dated, a combination pattern that was homely on the public side of the bar-counter but all chromium and black everywhere else and so completely characterless, or an edition of modern-ized Georgian. Whatever the choice, the large bar-room was part and parcel of the design. The Georgian solution, which has been labelled the 'Post Office' style, particularly emphasized the bare, bleak interior which denies the whole pub tradition and only succeeds in discouraging the customer from enjoying the modern equivalent of joining his cronies round the kitchen chimney corner. Admittedly much that was built was good competent architecture, but there was too much 'good taste' about it; far too much effort was spent on trying to build something that would not look like a pub.

So all of them lacked any sign either of the rural or of the urban vernacular and as a consequence passed over any suggestion that atmosphere was one of the most important qualities required in a pub.

The Road House type generally speaking is not a pub in the true sense and not usually owned by a brewery; but, nevertheless, like the wine bar they served a particular purpose, and they subsequently influenced the design of pubs not a little. They were aimed, like the city cocktail bar, at the 'bright young things' in the jazz age of the nineteen-twenties. They owed something to the tradition of the Gin Palace, quite a lot to the transitory spirit of their age, and frequently indulged the whimsies of both their promoters and their designers. Though pseudo-elements sometimes entered into them they were more often characterized by chromium and plastics, bright colours and display lighting. They often failed in their purpose, oddly enough, by not carrying the sense of illusion far enough, by being content to make half-hearted hints at it instead of going the whole hog. They failed, where the Gin Palace succeeded, by missing the decorative possibilities of their own stock in trade.

On analysis then, it is apparent that the pubs evolved by the brewers and their architects during the twenty years between the wars have not embodied the qualities that we find in many of the older pubs and which we would like to see reflected in the new. Instead, they are bleak, impersonal, barrack-like or pompous and self-conscious and lacking in intimacy or *bonhomie*. Even a good piece of architecture does not necessarily make a good pub, and although it is not suggested that good architecture should be abandoned, first and foremost it is good pubs that we want. A pub requires atmosphere of a certain specialized kind. Designing a bar functionally means catering for subtler human needs than convenience, durability, desire for display and need of supervision. The traditional pub satisfied these needs most effectively but the future pub will do no better than those described above, unless brewers and their architects accept the importance of the pub tradition, and, even more important, unless the magistrates admit that the pub is now a respectable place for respectable people and that their battle against the bad old days is won.

THE TRADITION REBORN

The pub tradition described in the second chapter has been broken, as the illustrations on pages 36–37 and 115–120 show. It must be re-established by contemporary designers if the modern pub is to be a real pub.

Having demonstrated, in the first place, that the pub has an important architectural tradition which, for a number of reasons, and in spite of its validity, has been allowed to disappear, and secondly, that in the absence of this tradition, the pub designer today seems unable to produce a really satisfactory pub, there can be little argument as to how the problem can best be resolved.

The pub, of all types of architecture, needs a tradition, because to enable them to feel part of a tradition is the best way of making people feel at home. But a tradition does not imply the conscious revival of previous styles; in fact, by definition it implies changing with the times. A contemporary pub must be a piece of contemporary architecture, and the question that arises is what can be learnt from the pub tradition illustrated on the preceding pages in order that the atmosphere so effectively created in the past can be re-created in a modern way.

Those illustrations make it quite clear that the things that are important about pub interiors are quite independent of the architectural styles current when they were built. The good Elizabethan pub is naturally typified by its old oak timbering and leaded lights just as the good Victorian pub is recognized for its characteristic carved mahogany and decorated glass. This contrast in style is, however, only superficial: their essential qualities are not just a question of their respective detail but derive from more deep-seated merits that are common to both. The next question, therefore, is whether it is possible to isolate the ingredients they have in common and decide whether they are still applicable today, so that modern architects can experiment in using them to produce a modern equivalent of the traditional pub interior.

Some of them can be defined without difficulty; barrels for instance. On page 39 barrels are seen displayed in a highly dramatic way that has rewarding possibilities. Barrels are acceptably modern forms. So are the repetitive effects obtainable from an array of bottles. They are the source of some of the most attractive pub interiors of many periods and a characteristic

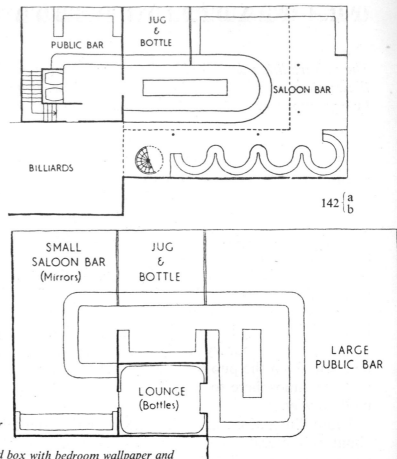

The Tradition Reborn. *The two hypothetical pub plans on this page and the drawings of the bars in them that follow are not intended to be complete solutions but they do show some of the potentialities of traditional pub decoration used in a modern way. In preparing them the guiding principle has been to use the materials to hand and with them to create character. The structure is contemporary, using the freedom of steel, concrete and glass. Paint, wood, lettering, mirrors, barrels and bottles are all materials or articles of common use. This is the beginning; with these materials the designer creates character suitable to a social place . . . intricacy, enclosure, mystery, brilliance and so on. How does this vary from your local? You will know the answer if your local has recently been redecorated and is now a naked box with bedroom wallpaper and fragile water colours in light oak frames, the whole bathed in pitiless fluorescent lighting. The plan (142a), shows a possible layout for a small Public Bar and a large Saloon Bar.*

The Public Bar may suggest an old pub, but it is a new one treated in a traditional way. The Saloon Bar has traditional Victorian features—space, semi-seclusion, decoration in equipment and broken vistas—but the form is modern.

The second plan (142b), shows a different arrangement from the first. It contains a smallish Saloon Bar, a large Public Bar and a Lounge Bar. The continuous bar-counter emphasizes on plan the spatial continuity seen in the drawing of the Public Bar, a continuity which is also emphasized by the mirror effects of the Saloon Bar. Each bar makes a point. The Saloon Bar shows an imaginative use of mirrors, the Public Bar adapts decorative devices normally more typical of the Saloon, while the Lounge Bar experiments with the decorative qualities of massed bottles and labels.

ingredient of the pub atmosphere, in that the effect of glitter they produce may well have been the starting point of the tradition of glittering and reflecting surfaces later built up in a spectacular fashion by means of cut and

(143) There is nothing in this small Public Bar deliberately modern or period. The materials, form and layout are functional. So if it looks like a bar you know, that is no reason why it should not also be a new bar. It was designed to be built with the materials to hand: wood, plaster, glass and paint. It is not extravagant or cheap but ordinary in the best sense. In its small space room is found for inner privacy in the high-backed seat. Once here you are out of the way and no one can stumble over your feet. The lower half of the window is screened. *Ceiling:* boarding painted high gloss white. *Walls:* painted teak. *Bar top:* zinc. *Bar front:* painted teak. *Seat:* light oak. *Table and floor:* scrubbed wood.

125

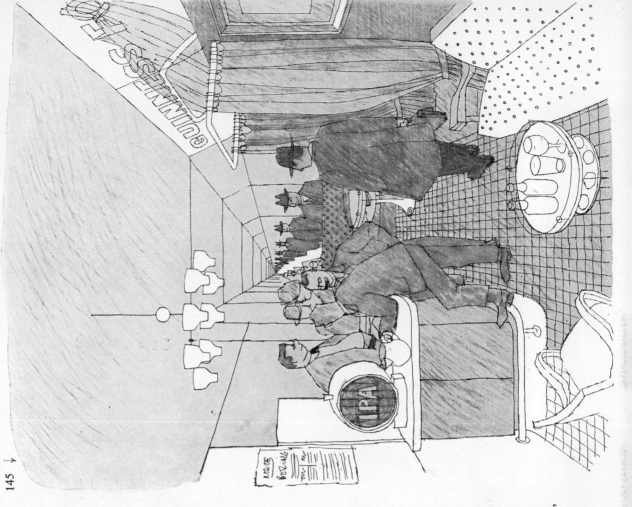

(144) The effect in this large Saloon Bar is the interplay of forms, volumes, and colours in a simple square box. While the box shape is preserved, its effect is partly offset by the use of an oblique mirror to bring the outside world inside, visible through a complication of lettering and light fittings. Meanwhile, the box extends itself on the left, down a long perspective of billiard tables. The volume is stressed by vertical pillars. Exaggeration of simple forms such as the hand, bottle and triangle gives incongruity. The flow of space is accentuated by the undulating banquettes and circular staircase. *Ceiling:* Lincrusta. *Walls:* glazed, mirror or advertising. *Bar-top:* mahogany. *Bar front:* cream. *Floor:* buff tile. *Furnishings:* red.

(145) The small Saloon Bar illustrates the uses of mirrors. It shows the simplest form of mirror trick, but there are many others, all too complicated to draw convincingly. Confusion for its own sake is hardly desirable in a public house, but the effects of space, the incongruity and the richness that can be achieved by mirrors are important for the designer. In a more complicated case, you might see, far in the dim recesses, perhaps inside the loop of a letter engraved on a distant mirror, a tiny arm which keeps moving up and down, and only after twenty minutes realize it is your own seen from behind.

127

(146) Reminiscent of the serial universe,
the large Public Bar starts by being real
and concrete but gradually dissolves into
mystery, an endless and intangible world of
barrels, pillars, lettering and mirrors. Once
again the functional interior. In essence the
room is just the space left below the first
floor of a building. It is glazed, the lower
part by obscured glass. Screens between
bars are mirrored and display the art of
the modern typographer and glass worker.
The bar-counter and fittings are all standard.
Ceiling: nicotine. *Columns:* chocolate.
Bar-top: zinc. *Bar front:* chocolate. *Floor:*
scrubbed boards. *Seats:* varnished plywood.

(147) This small and intimate Lounge Bar or Cosy (see plan 142b, page 124) shows, among other things, the use to which empties can be put. The walls and floor are relieved by lettering. It is not the 'novelty' of the arrangement which is interesting but the effects of repetition, intricacy, glitter, etc. Here, it must be stressed, the dangers of 'clever' interior decorating loom ahead, such as seats made from wine casks and so on. A word on furniture. Life on board ship owes much of its pleasure to the solidity of the furnishings. They have to withstand strain and movement. The same applies to the pub. Nothing is more annoying than a table which wobbles or is easily turned over. So if the tables shown here still trail clouds of cast-iron glory it is because no one has improved on the heavy, solid Victorian bar table with its railing and glass gallery below. *Ceiling:* Lincrusta varnished. *Walls:* bottles; teak below. *Floor:* carpet—something oppressively rich, maroon or damson. *Bar-top:* dark mahogany. *Bar surround:* natural mahogany. *Tables:* marble. *Upholstery:* black leatherette.

etched glass screens and mirrors. The decorative use of bottles obviously presents opportunities for the modern designer.

In many bar interiors even the bottles on the bar-back are reduced to a minimum, yet the decorative use of bottles obviously presents opportunities for the contemporary designer. So does the traditional pub's use of glass and mirrors, which also have their functional as well as their decorative origin. They help to create an atmosphere of seclusion without destroying the sense of space; by reflecting every movement they allow a solitary drinker to feel he is one of a crowd and the crowd in its turn appears to have more space at its disposal than it really has. Then there is lettering, type, and signals in general, from the Bass triangle and the Ind Coope hand to gilt ornamented brewers' names on the mirrors and the word RUM, or the brewers' advertisements and drink announcements. Much of this is easily incorporated into the modern interior. The false good taste that tears down engraved mirrors and puts up with plain rose-pink should be stopped at once. It is extraordinary that none of these aids to design were used in decorating the pubs of the inter-war period. The possibilities latent in bottles and mirrors, though they have so far been hardly exploited, are obvious; a more difficult study is the other more subtle elements of the best kind of pub character. Do natural materials create a more sympathetic effect than synthetic materials? Is there anything significant in the particular range of colours that the traditional pubs use? Here we come up against a principle of the first importance. Bar colours—chocolate, mahogany, teak, grained oak, buff, dark stone, light stone, cream—are highly stereotyped just because they have proved themselves sociable colours as well as useful. There is everything to be gained by taking them over and incorporating them in the modern bar, preferably in terms of paint (i.e. painted grained oak). The art shades of some of our present-day bars give any good pub-goer a pain. Again, do broken surfaces and intricate shapes assist the creation of a homely, sympathetic atmosphere, better than large unbroken surfaces and simple geometrical shapes? Does a sense of enclosure, combined with the feeling of something round the corner—or through the screen partition—by providing surprise and suspense, enhance the feeling of social well-being?

Many similar questions could be asked, but they can only be answered by architects trying out ideas as part of the process of actually designing pub interiors. As a graphic illustration of the possibilities latent in this approach to tradition, Gordon Cullen has made some drawings of a couple of hypothetical modern pubs. These must not be taken as a solution to the whole

131

problem but they do show some of the potentialities of traditional pub decoration technique when used in contemporary interiors. If architects would pursue the problem of pub design on these lines they could serve far better the interests of everyone concerned with pubs, but above all, those of the customer.

PUB COLOURS

Remember that pipe-smoke and varnish between them quickly bring all creams and whites to that pleasant and characteristic dark marmalade colour which is the best of all pub colours. Moving principle: don't repaint—revarnish, and so perpetuate the work of history and nicotine. Ceilings should always be varnished and so should all paint-grained surfaces and wallpapers. Varnish, layers of it, is the secret of success. Colours themselves are highly standardized—nigger, chocolate, mahogany, teak, dark oak, light oak, stone, buff, cream and white. Of these, teak (the paint) is probably most used, least 'known'.

Victorian Urban Saloon Bar

WALLS	Normally dark. Mirrors and panelled mahogany French-polished, or Lincrusta or mahogany graining (paint).
DADO	Normally dark. *Browns:* based on mahogany, nigger, chocolate. *Greens:* origin unknown, dark green, green/black. Usually low relief Lincrusta.
FRIEZE	Normally light. Cream, putty, buff, white with nicotine additions. Usually low relief Lincrusta.
CEILING	Light tones varnished. Plaster colours, pale cream; but always white with chocolate or nigger walls. Usually high relief Anaglypta. Sometimes low relief Lincrusta.
WOODWORK	Mainly dark. French-polished mahogany medium to dark tones.
FURNITURE	Wood: French-polished mahogany medium to dark tones. Metal: iron table supports and brackets. Brass. Marble.
UPHOLSTERY	Dark. Normally black leather or leather-cloth. Dark lime green and red plush; ditto for curtains behind the bar.
FLOOR	Normally dark. Anything from red Turkey carpet to pepper and salt mosaic.
ETCETERAS	Maroon, green and gilt spirit barrels. Dark or light brown casks, varnished. Copper and pewter pipes and pewter fittings to the bar. Sometimes even a pewter counter top. Mirrors with brewers' gilt lettering.

Country Pub Public Bar

WALLS	Medium to light. *Oak colours* for wood partitions light, medium, dark. Yellow-oak paint, brush- or comb-grained. Teak paint, light and dark.
CEILING	Normally light. Plaster colours, off-white, pale cream or buff washes. White with chocolate—sometimes teak paint—always highly varnished.
WOODWORK	Medium. Normally oak paint, brush- or comb-grained. Sometimes oak and teak combined. Mahogany or mahogany colours used also and sometimes combination of mahogany top and oak front.
FURNITURE	Light, medium and dark. Oak grained or teak painted. Natural scrubbed oak and deal frequent for settles and tables. Sometimes cream picked out in buff, sometimes nigger.
FLOOR	Medium and dark. Dark-oak stained or plain scrubbed deal.
ETCETERAS	Bottles, casks, containers and brewers' advertisements variegated.

BIBLIOGRAPHY

This list does not claim to be complete, but includes books that have been useful in providing material for this volume, certain textbooks on crafts which have a special place in pub design, and some literary works containing good descriptions of pubs in use.

ARCHITECTURAL AND SOCIAL

Thomas Burke: *English Inns* (Collins, 1944)

G. S. Chevalier: *Gavarni in London* (1849)

C. F. W. Dening: *Old Inns of Bristol* (Simpkin Marshall, 1943)

Charles Dickens: *Sketches by Boz* (1836)

Pierce Egan and George Cruikshank: *Life in London* (1821)

Maurice Gorham: *The Local* (Cassell, 1939)

Maurice Gorham: *Back to the Local* (Percival Marshall, 1949)

C. G. Harper: *The Old Inns of Old England* (Chapman & Hall, 1906)

Richard Keverne: *Tales of Old Inns* (Collins, 1939)

J. C. Loudon: *Cyclopædia of Cottage, Farm and Villa Architecture* (1833)

Elizabeth and Gilbert McAllister: *The Inn and the Garden City* (Batsford, 1948)

Mass Observation: *The Pub and the People* (Gollancz, 1943)

D. C. Maynard: *The Old Inns of Kent* (Philip Allen, 1925)

Basil Oliver: *The Modern Public House* (Westminster Press, 1934)

Basil Oliver: *The Renaissance of the English Public House* (Faber & Faber, 1947)

A. E. Richardson and H. D. Eberlein: *The English Inn, Past and Present* (Batsford, 1925)

A. E. Richardson: *The Old Inns of England* (Batsford, 1934)

H. Vizetelly: *Glances Back Through Seventy Years* (1893)

Whitbread & Co: *Your Local* (1947), *Inn-Signia* (1948), *Inns of Kent* (1949)

E. E. Williams: *The New Public House* (Chapman & Hall, 1924)

George B. Wilson: *Alcohol and the Nation* (Nicholson & Watson, 1940)

Francis W. B. Yorke: *The Planning and Equipment of Public Houses* (Architectural Press, 1949)

DRINKING

Anonymous: *A Vade Mecum for Malt Worms*

Thomas Burke: *Will Someone Lead Me to a Pub* (Routledge, 1936)

A. Drinker: *A Book about Beer* (Jonathan Cape, 1934)

William Juniper: *The True Drunkard's Delight* (Unicorn Press, 1933)

Frank A. King: *Beer Has a History* (Hutchinson)

André L. Simon: *Bottle-screw Days* (Duckworth, 1926)

CRAFTS

A. L. Duthie: *Decorated Glass Processes* (Constable, 1908)

J. P. Parry: *Graining and Marbling* (Crosby Lockwood, 1949)

A. V. Sugden and J. L. Edmondson: *A History of English Wallpaper* (Batsford, 1925)

Whitbread & Co: *Whitbread's Brewery* (1947), *The Brewer's Art* (1948), *Whitbread Craftsmen* (1948)

134